SOULPOETING

BENEDICT AUER, OSB

Soulpoeting
Healing through Poetry

ST PAULS

ST PAULS Publishing
187 Battersea Bridge Road
London SW11 3AS, UK

Copyright © ST PAULS 2000

ISBN 085439 593 8

Set by TuKan DTP, Fareham, UK
Printed by Interprint Ltd, Marsa, Malta

ST PAULS is an activity of the priests and brothers
of the Society of St Paul who proclaim the Gospel
through the media of social communication

Dedicated to
Our Lady of Lourdes
who heals the sick and infirmed,
the poor and brokenhearted,
and
Marcelline and William Auer,
Mother and Dad,
who have always shown compassion
not only to others but to me.

"Saintliness means living without division between word and action.
If I would truly live in my own life the word I am speaking, my spoken words would become actions, and miracles would happen whenever I opened my mouth."
Henri Nouwen

"What we have to be is what we are."
Thomas Merton

Acknowledgements

This book was a long time coming. But we never can write a book until we are mature enough to do so, and I hope I finally am. I have to thank my Benedictine monastic community of St Martin's Abbey for granting me permission and the funds for a year sabbatical in England. Abbot Neal Roth was instrumental in granting this permission and I thank him for realising I needed an extended break. Also four people who in their kindness wrote me and kept me informed the year I was away so I did not feel abandoned: Fr George Seidel, Br Lawrence Vogel, Br Boniface Lazzari, and Fr Kilian Malvey. I also have to thank my academic community of St Martin's College for allowing me a leave of absence from my position within the Education Division. I especially need to thank Dr David Spangler and Dr Joyce Westgard for expediting the process. This book would never have been written were it not for the Institute of St Anselm in Cliftonville, England. The programme under Fr Len Kofler, MHM, allowed me the chance to explore myself and reintroduce myself to the healing process of poetry. I especially wish to thank Sr Cecilia Goodman, IBVM, who inspired the first poems through her wonderful classes and deep insights into prayer. The 80 participants for the year 1998-1999 all played a part in this book, but especially Fr Thomas Lemp, a German Pallotine Father, Sr Marie Andre Shon, a Korean Benedictine from the United States, and Fr Antony Samy, a Claretian priest from India, whose friendship helped me through the rough spots. Finally I need to thank the man who walked me through this process, Fr Michael Doogan, a Scottish Passionist priest. His patience and compassion helped me gain control through poetry of my life.

While in England, I have to thank Holy Apostles Parish

in Pimlico, London in the Archdiocese of Westminster, and their pastor, Fr Robert Plourde. This parish served as my home base while in England. I need to thank all the parishioners, especially the Garwoods, Mary Hughes, Susanna Ridley, Eileen Sheedy, Jane D'Angelo, Nick Lane, the Millers, and so many more. Also I must mention my theatre companion and good friend, Fr Michael O'Boy. Also special thanks to my American family away from home, the Kennedy's – Mary, Peter, Will and Nicholas – who offered me the luxury of their home in Earith, England and included me in their family outings.

There are always special people who are there when you most need them. I am blessed with an abundance of intimate relationships that keep me sane. I would like to especially thank – Rob and Karen Kvidt, Jane Woolson, Josh and Dana Phelps, Loren and Sue Petty, Mark Bruso, and Rev Susanne Havlic. I am sure I have forgotten someone, but I appreciate all my friends. Finally this book would not have been possible without the support of my family. My dad and mother, William and Marcelline Auer, who have been an inspiration to me and helped me constantly with their support and were excellent parents. Also my sister, Mary, and my brother and sister-in-law, Dave and Alice Auer, who have always been supportive of my writing. I also have a wonderful niece and two nephews and their spouses, Holly and Michael Sorscher, David and Kathy Auer, and Joe Auer. And finally all my grandneices and nephews: Hannah, Nicholas, Samuel and Jacob William Sorscher and Jessica and Matthew Auer. Finally a special thank you to Tom Reichardt who took care of my mail, and did all sorts of needed things when I was away, and more important has been a good friend.

Contents

Introduction

Biblio/Poetry Therapy and Healing One's Life

Healing just doesn't happen. It is not accidental, but rather requires effort and intent. All of us are wounded. Our woundedness is often hidden deep within the recesses of our memory. Such memories defy excavation, first attempts meet with resistance and even interior hostility. Emotions are frequently repressed, and refuse to be dislodged. For some, years of therapy with an expensive therapist are the road to be followed. For others a less expensive path may be to ignore the pain and sorrow, and get on with life. But there is still a longing to address the issues which often escape and end up disrupting our lives. I believe there is an alternative to years of therapy or just getting on with life. I believe that the reading or writing of poetry, for some people who want to explore their lives and are not seriously troubled, is a good alternative.

The reading and writing of poetry has helped me cope with the many foibles and traumas in my life. It has helped me over the past fifteen years to confront issues in my life that have bothered me since early childhood. The writing of poetry has also helped me get in touch with my emotions and feelings. Poetry has been a good instrument for dislodging those feelings and fears that most of us have, but are peculiarly personal to each person. It took me almost fifteen years to finally write this book. Why? It is not a great earthshaking book. But I kept getting derailed along the way. I'd like to share with you this journey.

I was 46 when I wrote and published my first poem. Before that time I had read poetry and it had helped me, but not like writing a poem. My first poem erupted, the only word that might capture what happened, in print upon the page. It took me completely by surprise. During the first year I wrote over two hundred poems. More surprising was that publishers wanted to publish them. At first, I was hesitant because they were so personal. Some people called my poetry "confessional", but I called them "auto-biographical". Whatever they were, they were me. In 1986, my first book of poetry, *Touching Fingers with God*, was published by Winston-Derek Publishers. People wrote constantly about my poetry, letters saying how I touched their lives, sharing their experiences with me, and sometimes even poems.

But life went on. I continued to write poetry, publishing in over 250 magazines as well as two chapbooks of poetry. But slowly my new position as Campus Minister first, and adjunct lecturer in speech and religious studies, cut the flow of poetry to a trickle. Then I began studies for a Doctorate in Christian Spirituality in San Francisco. I wanted to tie up my poetry with Christian Spirituality. I did. It was difficult, much opposition from the Seminary staff, but finally I tied up poetry, spirituality, and prayer into a topic that eventually produced a dissertation entitled – "Deus Absconditus as Muse: An approach to the writing of poetry as a form of contemplative prayer for those who live with the hidden God". I took examples from the Bible (Psalms and Ecclesiasticus), Gregory of Nyssa, The Cloud of Unknowing, Thomas Merton, Karl Rahner and created a model for looking at poetry as prayer. Then I sounded off my model on Gerard Manley Hopkins, Rainer Maria Rilke, William Stafford, and other modern poets. Finally I produced 90 original poems. It worked and I got the doctorate. But still something haunted me. The thesis was over, but the process should be usable on a regular basis. It was not. I wanted to publish the dissertation, but it wasn't right. It was too academic. It was not user friendly. So it went to a shelf to collect dust.

But life went on. I became part of the Education Division of St Martin's College moving from Assistant Professor to Associate Professor. I developed courses on both the undergraduate and graduate level. I found a Catechetical Institute to train teachers and catechists from the Archdiocese of Seattle. And finally I burned out. Then something wonderful happened.

I was given a year, a monastic sabbatical, to recuperate from overwork, stress, and never saying no. I was accepted at the Institute of St Anselm in Cliftonville, Kent, England for their diploma course in Human Development and Religious Formation. I was exhausted. Life has lost much of its meaning. I was passive aggressive, emotional and mentally fragmented, and suffering from an acceleration syndrome or "driveness", always trying to do something more, never satisfied. At first when I arrived I dragged my feet, but slowly I realised that I was being given an opportunity that was wonderful – a chance to stop and re-evaluate what I had been doing with my life and rearrange for the better what remains of my life.

It was the coming of Sr Cecilia Goodman, IBVM, to the course to speak on prayer that triggered me to read and then write poetry again. And once again poems came pouring out, splashing upon the page, exposing my soul, and releasing feelings and emotions pent up over the years. I shared this poems with my facilitator and many participants in the programme from Europe, Africa, India, and many more countries. It helped many of them to see more clearly what was happening to them through my experiences. Then I recalled that this was the book I had wanted to write years ago, and had never written. The process was in place, the poems were written, and a format eventually came. I had taught children's literature back at the university. I had one section on bibliotherapy, and frequently students took topics dealing with poetry therapy. Somehow it all fell into place – my process was individual, but parts of it could be universalised. It was applicable to the man and woman in the street.

This book can be taken as my personal journey from

burn-out and psychological distress to wholeness, not complete, but on the road. But it is also a manual of suggestions for those who need or want to pursue a similar journey. Each chapter will have an introduction to a topic relevant to those who are trying to put their life back together, then a couple of poems that I have written on my personal journey , and finally a few questions to stimulate writing by the reader. It is not absolutely necessary that the reader write, my poems might be sufficient for a person to see that they are not alone on their journey through life. But hopefully the poet within each reader will be given permission to surface and articulate what cannot be spoken. Writing may free the interior person to speak in writing what would otherwise remain hidden.

This book is a do-it-yourself manual, but could be used in conjunction with a counsellor or therapist, or a spiritual director or a spiritual companion (I have included an article in Appendix II that gives an example of how this could be used in conjunction with one of the above people). But more than anything else, this is a book that freed me, freed me from the shackles of my childhood, my drivenness, and gave me back my life. Such a process may work for many of my readers. Poetry has a great ability to free. It is "inspired", breathed into a person. Often when the poem is done I realise that I did write it, something inside of me did, something more than myself. It is that thirst to be whole that gave me the title of this book *Soulpoeting*. My soul thirsts for God, for unity, for wholeness. This book of poetry self-therapy may help some of you to achieve this goal of integration.

One caution for the reader is that if the problem you are confronting in your life is really serious you need to go through this process with a professional or at least someone who can smooth out the rough spots. I did. Sometimes things surface and we do not even know they are there. It is at such times that we need someone to help us through the difficult spots. Keep that in mind.

Finally, I hope that you will use this book as a source of personal healing. I have written this book as a sharing exercise. Reading and especially writing poetry has freed me. It has "breathed" life back into a person deadened by fragmentation and "burn-out". I hope it can do the same for each of you.

Soulthirst

"Crazed by my soul's thirst...."

The Prophet by Pushkin
from a translation by Ted Hughes

Completeness
escapes me,
yearning enraptures
my innermost being,
I search endlessly
for something more
than what I have
or even am,
yet I know deep within me
that something is missing,
a small piece that makes
the jigsaw incomplete.
Parched from a thirst
that cannot be
quenched,
I drink in art,
music, literature,
spirituality,
but nothing seems to soothe
my dry throat,
my arid soul,
but I keep
thinking that
around the corner,

maybe even
in a deep recess of my mind,
I will quaff some elixir,
sweet and satisfying,
and finally
be satiated,
have the missing piece,
the puzzle
will be complete,
and finally I will have
peace.

Exhausted

*"Weary am I of my heart's bereavements,
and too old to put forth branches anew."*
Antoine de St Exupery

I'm tired,
and at times it is hard
to get up the enthusiasm
for even little things,
but that is only on bad days,
times when I only see the forest,
the trees undistinguished.
The forest is often sloe-coloured,
easy to get lost in,
yet on sunny days I can see
my way through the ebony undergrowth,
moleskin moss
fingers dunbark,
each olive leaf
clearly visible.
It is hard to live a paradox,
question marks replacing
exclamation points,
life on the edge of despair.

QUESTIONS

1. What would you like to change in your life if you could?

2. Do you feel like a "fake" or not genuine? What could you do to change that?

3. Does your life seem incomplete, lacking in wholeness? What could you do to change that?

4. Could you use poetry as a means of plummeting the deaths of your being? How? Read? Write? Both? Could you take a risk?

Chapter 1

"Glossolalia" with a Pen
[Inspiration and the Holy Spirit]

Poetry is a sacred art. The ancients considered the poet to be possessed by the gods. Even Karl Rahner, the German Jesuit, wrote an article on the priest as poet, and Thomas Merton, the American Trappist monk, considered his poetry as his most "God-filled" writing. Therefore before I start this book, I believe it is essential to make some statements about poetry and about inspiration.

The poetry we learned as children, namely poems that rhymed and had to be memorised is not what I am talking about. For me, poetry is speaking or writing with the heart. It is allowing language to speak through us and say what we are afraid to say. It is not about rhythm, rhyme, and meter, but about metaphor, image, simile, and feeling. It may be all of the above, but it may not be. But the concentration should not be on keeping a meter or trying to rhyme words, rather it is speaking soul onto paper. It was the poet Theodore Roethke who wrote "We think in feeling". And we do, but cannot articulate these deep feelings. So we are left with a build up of emotions within, and as Don Hannah wrote in his novel, *The Wise and Foolish Virgins*, "When you leave something behind it goes on without you". But in our emotional life, this may not usually be true. Those things do not go on, but we do with them. How do I get in touch with these feelings and emotions after ten or twenty or more years? Not easily is the answer.

In Selagh Stephenson's new play, *The Memory of Water*, a character asks "What do you plan to do?" And another character answers, "...live in the cold". We do not have to do that. Rather we can tap into our depths with poetry and touch our centre. We can read poetry and that will touch

21

our souls, but writing poetry is even better. It is like a drilling for oil, and striking a gusher. We spill out onto the paper. All that hidden deep black crude oil of our lives, our shadows, our pains, our hurts, puddles like a ink-blot psychological test onto the paper, and then we start to see who we are in the blotches before us.

Why is this chapter called "Glossolalia" with a pen? In the first years of the Christian era, the Holy Spirit came upon the early believers and they spoke in tongues or Glossolalia. I believe that poetry is inspired. The word "inspiration" is from "to breathe into". The Spirit or spirit breathes into each of us. We cannot articulate what has happened to us in words alone, but all of a sudden we speak in tongues. Now writing may be threatening to some of us. Can I do this with other people's poetry. Yes. But keep an open mind. You too can write poetry.

So poetry is a form of prayer. Grace Schulman, the former poetry editor of *The Nation* and a brilliant poet, once asked me if I did not think that poetry was prayer, and real prayer poetry. I agreed readily. I find that writing poetry frees me to speak my soul, and sometimes that is an energising experience. My pen says what my mouth cannot. My pen or rather my computer often becomes spirit-possessed. Images flow into metaphor, while metaphor captures the inarticulate idea or feeling.

Finally sometimes we expect order out of our lives. Sorry. I haven't found it, but maybe you will. I have found paradox. My life, if nothing else, has been paradoxical. When I think I am in control, I discover I am not. When I find peace, it is accompanied by chaos. Anachronism, coupled with paradox, seem to be my middle name. But I have come to accept that as part of my humanness. So don't fear poetry, but rather embrace poetry only as a reader if it seems too overwhelming, and then hopefully as a writer. Remember the spirit opens our hearts, our minds, and finally our souls. It is a risk, but not one-sided, somehow God plays a role in all this.

Muse Fear

"A single surge has swept me from myself."

Hippolytus in Racine's *Phedre*

Asked where
the words come from,
I often say
"Not from me",
people accuse me
of false modesty,
but it is absolutely true.
I fear
the poetic muse,
overpowering
my senses,
stealing my eyes,
ripping my brain,
eventually
possessing me.
I type my soul
on to a screen,
computerising
words that speak
beyond me,
my fingers
often hunt and peck
while touching
fingers with God.
Poetry is
a humbling experience,
words ooze
out of my pores,
my mind goes non-stop,
I birth letters
that spawn words
that speak
of something beyond me.

I fight
the poetic urge,
until I succumb,
then soul
touches paper
and I disappear.

Why do I Poet?

"Last night, eighty-four thousand poems.
How, how make them understand?"
Layman Stoba (1036-1101), Zen poet

My mind
never stops,
unfolding poem
after poem,
after poem,
until I have heard
my story
over and over again,
yet it goes on
exploring nooks and crannies
that have long grown dusty,
past events, persons,
and even things.
I write pain,
find words to articulate
in black and white
what was once prismatic,
colours sucked either/or,
no shades, no pastels,
just ebony and ivory.
Computer literate
means more to me,
my typewritten life
takes shape and form,

words seem to speak
of sense and sensibility,
covering over absurdity,
on paper life is concrete,
not abstract,
people may not agree,
but sometime they may understand,
if not me,
themselves.

Blood into Ink

*"But he was right that to the degree a writer has
metamorphosed his blood into ink his is an
abandoned body."*

Edmund White, *The Farewell Symphony*

Blood
drips from my fingertips,
the computer keys
run dark crimson
as my soul seeps
onto the screen,
life force suspended
between self and screen,
laptopping my story
in recited alphabet,
allowing God
to make sense
out that which
I call my life.
Slowly words
take on more meaning,
a clearer definition,
than the experience,
possibly more than
life itself.
My fingers type messages

having touched
digits with God,
shadows of me,
spooky illusions
ghosted in metaphor,
I spill out so much of me
that my body feels abandoned,
an empty shell tortoised
slow motion by my reluctance
to deep dive,
afraid of the depth,
yet shining light into crevices
that hold encrustations
older than me,
passed ancestrally,
from mother to mother
and finally son.

QUESTIONS

1. Do you feel comfortable risking putting the pen to paper and touching "fingers" with God? Maybe not yet. Then write down anything that after reading the poems before these questions that touched you. Any idea? Don't worry, just write.

2. Are there poems within you? Do you think you could allow one to come out? Try it.

3. Is your life paradoxical, if so why? If not, explain why?

4. Pick up the pen and try to write something about a hidden feeling. What metaphor could describe it? What image best conveys you?

Chapter 2

Waiting without Soul

[A starting point]

Getting started is the hardest part. Where do I start? What do I do? I haven't been in touch with who I am for years. Now what? I felt that way a few years ago. Everything I wanted had happened. I had been promoted to Associate Professor of Education. Been elected as a member of the Society of Fellows. I had spoken at three national conventions that year – social studies, archaeology, and computers. I had published my usual three articles in magazines. I had founded a Catechetics Institute that was going very well. Yet I felt hallow, empty. Nothing made sense.

I found myself without anything left. I had gotten to where I wanted to be, and my major question was "So what?" I felt soulless. I was driven, but what had it gotten me. I couldn't sit still, and I certainly did not want to be with myself. But where did I start. I needed some inspiration. But I wasn't even listening. I was running. I was actually fleeing from myself.

I started my sabbatical with the feeling I had been shafted. Hoodwinked into joining a programme that propertied to be a training ground for formation leaders, and here it was saying things like "You have to start with yourself". I was hurt. I was a victim. But then I sat down and tried to take part in the programme. Then one day, Sr Cecilia Goodman came and talked to us. She told us a story about the Aborigines in Australia who do a walkabout, actually a runabout. Running and running until exhausted by the run, they fall to the ground in order to let their souls catch up to them. It hit me right between the eyes. It catapulted down into my very being. I recognised myself. I was sitting waiting for my soul to catch up to me. It was a revelation.

I found myself shocked. I recognised in an instant that I was a monk who prayed without depth, rather I was praying by rote. I was a professor who taught on sheer will power. I no longer loved what I did. It wasn't because what I did was bad, but it no longer had meaning for me. I had burnt out before, but never so drastically. Life had lost its meaning, but even will power was failing me. It had all become imbalanced. What was important was no longer. I was into the details, but the overall meaning was lost. I tried to catch my breath.

At that moment, I stopped. It was for the first time in twenty years. I was a person who had done a Master of Arts degree that was supposed to take two years in one, a Master of Divinity that was to take four years in two and a half, and finally a Doctorate, while teaching full time, so quickly that my monastery did not have the tuition paid yet. I wrote a dissertation of 260 pages in less than three weeks, and it was accepted with minor corrections. But I had lost the meaning. It was at that moment when I had to stop and say "What does it all mean?"

I couldn't answer my own question. I just sat and cried. It was then I started to write poetry. I started to realise that in the ten or fifteen years I might have left of my productive life I wanted to be me, not someone I wanted people to think I was. It was that moment I stepped into the abyss, and let go. It was then that poetry erupted from my very soul.

Often we need such an event. Desperation. A death. A rejection. A realisation. Something that speaks to us so existentialistically that we can do nothing but utter an "Angst". A scream into the air that echoes the pain etched into our souls. That is the starting point. That is when poetry can be written, maybe even using our blood, not literally, to write our metaphors for survival. At that point, we will be willing to listen to our inner spirit, our soul. It is then that we write not words, but feelings and even what I called *soulscript*, writing that only the soul knows how to do.

One thing to remember is that we have to attune our ears to hear. The voice of God is silent, or at best a gentle breeze or whisper. And if our life is too loud, we drown out the very voice of God. In *Dead Poet's Society*, the students bring a telephone to the assembly, and then they let it ring. The headmaster looks around, and one of the students says "It's for you, it is God calling." That sadly doesn't happen for most of us. The call to stop, or come to a full stop, is often so soft we will miss it if we do not attune ourselves to the whisper. I found that it took a major intervention, and then a full stop, and finally a few words at the right moment to jump start my life once again.

Waiting without Soul

"Aborigines sometimes run for days until exhausted, then sit and wait for their souls to catch up to them."
Sr Cecilia Goodman, IBVM

In the time before dawn,
CD Chanting
Buddhist monks and nuns
blend their mantras
as I sit
waiting for my soul
to catch up to me
on the coast of England.
As an American
I ran too fast
for my soul
to keep even parallel
with me
so now
I sit soulless.
Yesterday I did a mandala
that spoke to me
through tears,
but couldn't yet

penetrate my inner heart.
Lacking in trust,
I also fail the patience test
for I try to speak
words without meaning,
words without soul, heart.
The wait seems
overly long,
but I have switched
from my time
to Godtime,
I now have all time –
slow down heart,
sit patiently and wait.
A soft, yet divine whisper
may soon
glance kisslike
off my cheek.

A True Philosopher

*"True philosophers are those who embark upon a voyage
into the unknown, unsure of their destination or
whether they might even return."*

James Cowan, *A Mapmaker's Dream*

The sea
was angry today,
throwing itself
against the shore
with suicidal intent,
only to pull back
before annihilation,
but the feigned death
was not for me,
rather I was only
a voyeur
not a participant

30

in act of madness.
October hail fell
with huge tear drops,
forcing me to shelter,
as if mocking
my timid attempts
at introspection,
dwarfing my petty rages,
knowing full well
I stand at the abyss,
not the sea's,
but my own.
The voyage
will be worse
than if I embarked
in this October storm,
for mine has been
roaring much longer,
not a half hour,
but a lifetime,
lashing my interior beach,
my risk much greater,
not just to body,
but possibly my very soul.

Recognising the Voice

"God is always at home.
It is we who have gone out for a walk."

Meister Eckhart

In the film
Dead Poet's Society,
a student pretends
to get a phone call
during morning assembly.
When the phone rings,
he answers it

and tells the headmaster
that it is God calling.
I have spent
the majority of my life
waiting for that ring,
putting my life
on hold,
sitting through
sleepless nights
waiting as if
for Godot,
but I only get
wrong numbers
or solicitors.
Each ring
I anticipate
a divine voice,
hoping beyond hope
that this time it is God,
but then it is
a lonely voice
or a distraught student,
and again
I missed God,
or did I.
I wonder if maybe
I have heard
from God,
but just haven't
recognised the voice.

QUESTIONS

1. What would it take to jump start your life? What major intervention is needed? Or can you do it now?

2. What do you need in order to open up your inner-most self, and allow it to surface? Can reading poetry help? Can you make a list of what you need to do?

3. Have you left your soul behind? Can you stop to allow it to catch up?

4. Will you try to articulate in words or metaphors how you feel about your life? What do you need?

Chapter 3

Giving Oneself Permission
[To be, not to do]

My undergraduate and my first Masters degree in history were taken under the Jesuits. You probably will say that explains a lot. It does. But it is not their fault that I am as I am. There message was that each of us could effect the world around us if we gave our life to the Christian message. You never took second best, but went for first, and if you got second prize, it is better than if you went for third or fourth prize. Somehow this philosophy got perverted within my mind. I took it in and with it a perfectionism that was inordinate. I wanted to be perfect. I had an uncle who was a Jesuit who we kidded had never made a mistake in his life. But the point is I put myself on overdrive, and eventually defined myself with what I did, and not who I am.

It is true that each of us has a strong desire to accomplish something with our lives, to live a legacy of some kind for the world. That is not bad. We want to leave something behind when we die. We want to write a book. We want to build a church. We want to create an invention that will change the world. We want to win a medal at the Olympics. It is not a "five minutes of fame" syndrome, but rather we would like to truly change the world for the better. Now up to that point that was the Jesuit philosophy of education. It was giving our lives for Christ. It is excellent.

But now for the perversion. Henri Nouwen put it quite well when he wrote "...we start being too impressed by the results of our work, we slowly come to erroneous conviction that life is one large scoreboard where someone is listing the points to measure our worth". That is what happened to me. And it can happen to many of us. I defined myself with what I did, not who I am. Doing is not being. But to reverse that being can include doing, but not just doing. God became for me the ultimate scorekeeper. It was a kind of Pelagianism, "earning my salvation". I felt that I could get God's attention by doing more and more. Not just being who I was. But who I am is what God ultimately loves. I, even as a monk and priest, was in the world, and of the world. I had lost my perspective. I started to measure my life by my successes, and eventually they were never good enough.

The first thing I had to do was to break this vicious cycle, and it was vicious or maybe insidious. I had already stopped, but now I had to take charge of my life. First, I took charge of the programme I was in, and evaluated what I needed from the programme and what I did not. I stopped attending classes just to please the instructor, and made it clear in my own mind that I did not need more knowledge for the sake of knowledge. I rather needed to be in control. I had ultimately to give myself permission to be who I am. And who I am is good enough. I didn't need more degrees or more articles or more anything to be loved by God. I was loved.

This did not happen overnight it was a slow process, and will continue the rest of life. Patterns of behaviour are hard to break or change. But by writing it in black and white, it became real for me. I knew it was what I had to do. It was giving myself permission to be, not to accomplish. I didn't need one more anything. I just needed to be. I find it interesting that when God was asked to define himself by Moses, God didn't give a job description. Instead, God simply said "I am who am", another translation is "I am". The closer we can come to that definition the more we are like God. But that is a lifelong struggle and not one accomplished overnight. We have to combat our insecurity, our fears, our lack of trust, and so forth. We were not really born with those attitudes and feeling, although some psychologists now say we had the propensity from the womb. Rather we developed them through years of practice, and so shedding them will not be easy. Poetry helps us give ourselves permission to do so. Reading it gives us ideas and writing frees us or at least exposes our innermost self. I had to see in black and white, on printed paper, that I now had permission to be, and even though I still might do, being was more important. Out of my being, or my "I aming", my doing would now flow. If not always at first, at least more frequently, and in the long run, my life would start to gain some balance.

Giving Myself Permission

"Now this famous pride is crying for help."
Hippolytus in Jean Racine's Phedre

Thirty *Who's Who* volumes
with my name next
to David Attenborough
and the novelist Atwood,
I still can't give myself
permission
to miss a class.
Unsure at fifty-nine,
uncertain at eight,
life slips through
my palm lines,
midlife turns
into senior citizen,
yet I can't say
"Go for it."
Instead,
I pursue replication,
duplicating what
I don't need,
afraid to miss
what I already know.
My mouth says

"Permission granted"
but head
won't allow it,
maybe afraid
that I will miss
the voice of God
in the ordinary
repetition of
mundane fact.
Today maybe
heart and mind
can utter
"Permission granted"
by accepting
the me who I am,
and forgetting
the persona
I have created.

Inner Conflict

*"Travelling towards the light
we were waylaid by darkness."*

R.S. Thomas

I have always
wanted to be
like everyone else,
just normal,
nothing special,
yet a secret voice
keeps saying
"You are unique",
always countered
by another voice
shouting
"No, you're not."
Other children

played baseball,
I read books;
adolescents
hated writing,
I loved poetry;
young adults
danced,
I listened to Opera;
adults
can't understand kids;
I do;
the elderly
look to retirement;
I see a new career.
Normality
seems to have
passed by my crib,
missed my adolescence,
and completely
turned its back
on my adulthood.
Now I must reconcile
this conflict –
unique is ok,
normal is terminal ennui.

QUESTIONS

1. How can I give myself permission to be? Do I need to do so? If so, why?

2. "Permission granted" may sound like a simple statement, but what does it do for you? How do you feel when you say that to yourself?

3. How do I define myself? Give a metaphor that might describe that definition? Write a poem that might articulate who you are ? To yourself? To others? To God?

4. Give yourself permission to be. How does that feel? Capture that feeling on paper

Chapter 4

My Monsters
[Finding our fears]

Each of us is ghosted by our own monsters. These feelings or attitudes affect all we do. They scare the living daylights out of most of us. We can deny them until we have no breath but to no avail. Some therapists say to befriend them, but how can we befriend what we do not know. Often these feelings are repressed, residing in a nether world deep within ourselves. So how do I get in touch with these monsters.

First of all, caution is important. Our feelings can overwhelm us. But poetry can slowly release a few of these feelings: anger, fear, anxiety. As they are released and written down on paper, they can be handled. If it can be written down, it is controllable or changeable. It is now manageable. If a fear can be put into words, it is not as frightening as when it is a ghosted, overpowering presence surfacing into our life explosively. For instance, many of us are angry. But it is suppressed. So we may put up with instances that are horrific. We may not loose our temper over affronts and abuses, but one day someone asks us to open the door and we explode. We are shamed. We feel totally in the control of this anger. But when I write down this episode, I realise the request to open the door is not the thing I was angry about, rather it was only a trigger. But now I start to look at what really triggered the event. Maybe my constantly being put upon by others. Then I allow my poet-ego to write about my "being constantly put upon by others". I realise that metaphors come up, some trite: doormat, punching bag, and so forth. Finally, I start to articulate in words how I feel. I feel like a punching-bag. A simile but a start. Then slowly an image merges. I am a punching bag

41

for the people who surround me. The experience becomes a feeling. I am pummeted. I am abused. I have started to allow to surface the issue. Poetry slowly frees me to see and articulate the hidden. I throw light on the shadow part of me. These are my monsters.

Second, I start to see that many of my fears are ridiculous. I am a tenured professor yet at times I feel threatened in my position. I rationally know that I would really have to do something totally inappropriate to be removed from my position, but I still can be anxious. If I put it on paper, poet the feeling, I realise the fear or anxiety is silly. Now I see it in perspective. It is real, but it is unreal. I then can address the issue in words, in image, in metaphor. Why am I really afraid or fearful?

Third, poetry can be safe too. I mean poetry concretises a phantom. I see what is really happening, but often in symbolic language. It may be the only way to state the unstatable. Fear can control my life. Poetry can release the chains, or at least untighten them. I can't address an issue if I really don't know what it is. If I keep having explosions about ordinary things and write it off, and never address the situation, I will never find out the root, only keep worrying about the symptoms.

Finally, my monsters will not go away, but slowly we may placate them or even befriend them. My anger may be able to be rechannelled. It is a powerful energy within me. That energy can create powerful poems, poems that explode onto the page. Or it may be that this energy will be challenged into really addressing issues that deserve our anger – world hunger, misuse of the environment, and so forth. On paper, an anger out of control or totally repressed can surface and be spotted for what it is, namely, a monster who needs to be tamed. Taming our monsters is really naming our fears and anxieties. In the Old Testament, God never gave his name, even to Moses, "I am who am" is not God's name. Why? Because in the Middle East and in ancient cultures, giving of one's name was giving another person control. So naming still has the connotation of control. We control that which we can name. Naming gives us awareness, and awareness is half the battle. At least, now I know. I may not be able to do something about it immediately or even quickly, but slowly as my awareness grows, I gain control of my life. Naming our monsters gives us a leash to put around its collar. Slowly we can train that monster to be controllable, recognised, but on its good behaviour. Released to play, but only on my terms, not the monsters'. A poem may start that process.

My Monsters

"To enact the work we believe in, to protect the people and places we love, to follow the path we know is ours demands a constant engagement with scary, unfamiliar demons. We match this monster not with weapons, but with self-knowledge."
Trebbe Johnson, "The Monster of Grim Prospects"

> On the outside
> of medieval
> world maps,
> the cartographer
> etched:
> "Beware of Dragons."
> I have scribbled
> the same message
> on the edges
> of my life.
> My dragons
> are multiple,
> but all stem
> from fear,
> or maybe
> a lack of trust.
> Beware
> may be

my middle name,
written
with the fearful voice
of my mother,
steeped in
the early death
of my father.
Anxiety
raises its head
above the clouds
into my secure ivory tower,
shaking my confidence,
rupturing my world,
until I hide behind
my persona,
a face mask
created to ward
off demons,
to scare away monsters,
to slay undying dragons.
Yet they keep coming,
these Halloween goblins,
slipping into my dreams,
pursuing me with daymares,
scaring me
with Jungian shadows.
I am exhausted
from the fighting,
for myth is hard
to defeat,
especially when
one considers
one's life
a fiction,
autobiographical,
but a fiction
anyway.

I should
rescript the story,
refocus the plot,
repoet the verse,
if that is impossible,
then I must
settle for awareness,
second best,
but maybe
for a little while
I can put down the sword.
Victory is not winning
the battle,
but learning the strategy
to survive.

A Beach on the South Channel near Margate

*"Show me the face you had before even your parents
were born."*
Hui Neng (8th century), Buddhist sage

Surging sea
touches my shoes,
each reoccurrent wave
lapping the shore
with stolen kisses
and then retreating
back to the sea.
Along the shore,
I discover Zen gardens
hollowed into the rocky shore,
small stone pools
in which God has arranged
pebbles in never repeating patterns:
two perfectly rounded off-white stones
with a small ebony stone
intimately snuggled,

45

as if a family,
while two shells
without their original inhabitants
lay nearby
with beautifully etched
circular whirlpool designs
in shades of brown.
Shafts of sunlight play
on the water
creating
a rainbow prism
that radiates
on to the next pool,
and the next,
my mind easily overloads
and like the sea
I too have to retreat
from the shore
fearful I will want
to stay and gaze
at each pool
until my reflection
narcissus-like
would never let me go
beyond the present moment.

Words

*"Talking: seven steps, eight falls.
Silent: tripping once, twice."*
Shishin-Goshin (c1339)

I walk carefully
with words,
my verbal crutch,
which helps me abuse
those whom I love.
Syllables carom off

the back of my mind,
I talk not to clarify,
or even inform,
but rather because
I have to –
it proves I am.
Each word
chain reacts
into new words,
spontaneous combustion
in a world gone mad.
Nervously I continue
to speak in riddles
the meaning of life.

QUESTIONS

1. What monsters play in your depths? Name them.

2. Take one of these monsters and allow it to surface.
   Now pick a metaphor to describe the monster. Play
   with the metaphor. You are in control.

3. Take a walk. Observe your environment. Now pick
   an image that you wish to describe and try to describe it on paper. Does the image mean more than
   what it is? If so what does it mean?

4. Write a poem about your monsters or monster. Don't
   worry about form or anything else only articulating
   the monster. What metaphor or simile can describe
   this "ghost" ?

Chapter 5
Nothing Makes Sense
[What is it all for?]

When I finally stopped running, I found that my life didn't make sense any longer. I had relativised my entire life, everything was equal. I no longer knew what was important, and what wasn't. In fact, the only way to describe the sensation or feeling was "Nothing makes sense". My question was "Why?" I was going through the motions on many a day. There were good days, but many were colourless and without meaning. We always laugh at our academic robing service when our registrar reads off the colours and for the business degree it is drab. But drab was my colour.

Life had lost its vitality. Without meaning life is not worth living. But my life had meaning or did it? T.S. Eliot in *The Lovesong of J. Alfred Pufrock* writes "I measured my life in coffee spoons". I don't drink coffee, but my life seemed just as meaningless. I had wanted to be accepted as a theologian, but instead I was a professor of education. I wanted the academic recognition, but now within college circles education professors are looked at as professional preparers, and not academics. I worked hard at what I did, but even the Academic Vice President referred to our division as a vocational programme. But that was not the real problem, the real issue was that it all seemed so useless and unnecessary.

I didn't want to play the game any longer. My identity was in what I was doing, but more than that I felt meaningless. My religious life was imbalanced because I taught evenings and missed Mass and Vespers with the monastic community at least twice a week. I felt unappreciated. Commonly referred to by community members as a workaholic which hurt me deeply, but it didn't seem anyone cared.

49

My mother who usually gives me sound advice said, "Can't you be satisfied with what you got?" My answer was "No". But I felt boxed in, and didn't have the means to release myself.

Later, when I was writing poetry to make sense out of my life, I realised that I had completely identified with what I was doing, and when that was attacked so was I. I couldn't separate the two. Like an alcoholic, I needed to get as low as I could so that the only way was up. When I left on my sabbatical I was there. I needed a change, a drastic alteration. Given the opportunity I would have chosen another degree. Luckily, I didn't go that route. Rather I was pushed into a situation where I was forced to confront the only person with the answers, namely me. Life didn't make sense or have meaning because I had allowed it to develop that way. I could blame thousands of others, both living and dead, but when it came down to an answer, the answer was already in me.

My poetry spelled out an answer, but first it raised the question: Why does nothing make sense? The answer was simple, the correction was more complex. I had to give my live meaning again, and it was not in accomplishments and degrees, in articles or books, but buried deep within me. I had to accept myself. I knew I couldn't keep going, but once I stopped could I ever get going again. So I stood at the edge of a precipice, looking into the void below, but afraid that I might fall into the unknown.

It was an interesting image for me. I loved the Scripture statement that says to "fall into the hands of God". I remember a story I was told years ago about a child who was seen by a man walking on a roof of a tall building. The child walked to edge of cliff seemingly unafraid and stood there and smiled at the man. And then he jumped. The man screamed. He then ran to the edge. And there the youngster was in the hands of his father into whose hands he had jumped. The object of that lesson is that we can jump into the hands of God, a loving Father, but it does take faith and risk, but more important a belief that God will catch us. I didn't at that stage have that kind of faith any longer. I liked the Scripture quote, but it was beyond my comprehension at that stage in my life.

Poetry at least helped me to identify how I felt, and possibly some paths to take. But answers weren't readily available nor can they be. Simple answers to complex questions usually do not work. So I identified the problem, and that was sufficient.

Nothing Makes Sense

"The Word was made flesh through love."

John Duns Scotus

A first grade teacher
knows all about original sin
through first hand experience,
her charges are not cherubic,
daily flawed nature
confronts her,
imperfection is evident,
yet other times
each child seems sinless.
Human nature is
ultimate paradox,
nothing about mankind
is black or white,
grey permeates
the landscape
of our minds,
we contradict
even as children
who we are.
Duns Scotus
had too simple an answer,
so did Meister Eckhart,
and in recent years

Matthew Fox –
we are unfallen,
Jesus died because
of a lark on his Father's part,
yet my senses contradict
this heresy,
flawness is everywhere,
crippled from birth,
never whole,
always fragmented.
The heretics speak
words that seem comforting,
but paradox effects
these very words,
salvation without crucifixion
drops the paradoxical nature
of such a gift,
then nothing makes sense.

Shades of Self

"At times I love the knife that wounds me."
Robert Sabatier

Evening shadows criss-cross
sprigs and tendrils,
meadow grass,
and even the willow
that shades the cattails
that hug the marsh ends,
finally the spectrum of dusk
even shades me.
I sit along the bank
toying with the broad leaves
of the bur-reeds,
stripping the dark brown furry pods
off the nearby cattails,
waiting for deepening twilight

to swallow up everything in sight.
I should go but remain
darkness envelops the bog,
deepening the algae:
lime becomes olive,
then deep charcoal green.
I fear such pigmental change
and realise that I can darken my soul
with the ease that the withdrawing sun
removes its light from this swamp,
for I cannot rid myself of all the traces of
guilt,
I darken my soul to ebony
as quickly as night gobbles up eventide.

Amazing Journey

"Life is not a straight road; often it is more like a maze."
Gerard Egan, The Skilled Helper

Nothing is clear,
the glass is etched
with the breath of fear,
reason is sitting
in the rear seat,
feelings grasp
at the wheel,
the car is definitely
not in my control.
I know the way,
driven it often enough,
yet today it seems
somehow mistaken,
landmarks are not
supposed to be there,
the car seems
to be driving itself,
haven't I passed

that way before,
shouldn't I turn
at that monolith,
no longer sure,
Auden poems play
in my mind,
"O where are you going
said reader to rider."
My route no longer straight,
rather every direction
seems better,
trapped in a maze of no direction,
I circle myself,
afraid to stop,
I'd never be able
to accelerate to this speed again,
so I go on,
and on,
and on.

QUESTIONS

1. Does your life have meaning, or do you feel as if everything is meaningless at times? Does your life make sense?

2. What did give your life meaning? Could you recapture that, and how?

3. Write a poem that addresses this issue of meaning? Pick words that you find meaningful and tie them together in reaffirmation of your life. If you can't think of any then choose those that you would like?

4. Try to choose a metaphor, e.g., a path, a pilgrimage, etc. Now write a poem to see if you can tap into meaning or how to find meaning for your life.

Chapter 6

Transparency
[Fragility and vulnerability]

I realised for the first time in my life while I was trying to come in touch with myself by doing poetry that I was a very fragile person. Vulnerability is a difficult thing for some of us to accept. I thought I was strong, but in fact my strength was a mirage, not real only an illusion. In reality I was extremely fragile. But most surprisingly, at least for me, I discovered most people are fragile. We break easily, sometimes surviving simply by perseverance. We heal slowly.

I had built walls around myself to protect me from hurt. I felt that at any moment I might break. Who could I tell this to? Would anybody understand? I worried that I might be having a breakdown. Could I confront myself and still survive? This was a period of great confusion for me.

Something that was important to me from this period was that poetry could help me express my woundedness. What I could not say to another person I could say in poetry. The words could express what I felt while I could not say those feeling by mouth, at least pen could articulate them. When I shared these poems with others, they would say "I know what you mean" or "I feel the same". It was this community of wounded people that assured me I was not alone. I was not the first person ever to experience this fragility.

It was extremely painful. I hurt physically, mentally, emotionally, and even intellectually. And without being too dramatic, I felt totally abandoned. I had to go through all this by myself. No support. Yet I did have support from my family, friends, and community members. Many were oblivious, but many commiserated with me. Many people helped me through this time. On the one hand I felt transparent, fragile, and vulnerable, needing support, but on the other hand, I was afraid people would see me this way. It was then I realised life is a paradox. What I wanted and needed was scary because I was seen not as who I wanted people to see me as, but as I am. Such a paradox is the human condition.

When I taught high school English, I used to have my 14-year-old students read a William Carlos Williams short story about a young girl who the doctor thought had diphtheria. The doctor had to try to get her to open her mouth. Finally forcing a spoon into her mouth so that he could see her throat. The doctor became almost subhuman during this episode. I used to point out to my students that we are each like that doctor. We are two circles one which is who we are, and one which is who we show to others. And these two circles seldom are on top of each other, rather during most of our lives, the circles overlap only slightly. We are actually two different people, and as you will see later actually many different people.

It was at this stage that I realised I had two choices – to accept who I was or go on living my "masked" existence, a life without meaning. It really came home to me when I discovered that it was my sixtieth year. At sixty, I might have another ten or fifteen years left of academic teaching at most. Many of my friends had retired at the age of 55. Some were already dead. How did I want those last ten years or so to be spent? In isolation, or as a vulnerable person. I decided that who I was was much more important to me than my positions or degrees. So I was able to acknowledge my fragility. When people look at my life now and say, "What a wonderful series of successes you have had. You must be very pleased." I answer "Yes I am, but now I realise that I am very fragile." Any real progress I make must be based on the fragility or I will go back to being the way I was.

Poetry has helped me accept this fragility and vulnerability. I would like to have people say of me eventually

"He did a lot, he contributed a lot, but he was human, vulnerable." What I guess I am aiming at is transparency. People will be able to see through me and what they will see is good. Actually what I am seeing is that I am good, much better than I thought. Poetry has helped me address that issue.

Metaphoric Fragility

"What we have to be is what we are."

Thomas Merton

I
metaphor my life,
poeting each moment,
seeing through flesh
into soul,
seeing tears
in each rainfall,
a rainbow
in a sunlit snowflake.

I
speak words
that become pictures,
photographing
minus camera,
but photo
turns to x-ray.

I
see too much,
my soul
replaces skin,
rubbed rough
by soft air.

I
feel
so fragile,
wondering
if survival
is possible
even for another day.

A Poet in puris naturalibus

"The meaning is in the writing."

R.S. Thomas

I am typewriting
my soul on paper mirrors,
opaque self-images
which Morse code a story
so old it creaks ennui.
I spume tales
about events
which mean something
only to me and my muse.
Myths unwind.
I voyeur my mind,
unshadowing the unspeakable,
flashing words which
expose my heart
to public view,
leaving me
a lonely nude,
a poet in puris naturalibus.

Humble Transparency

"In receiving the guest as Christ, a Benedictine is standing before Christ in humble transparency."

Columba Stewart, OSB

I seem
at times to be fading,
shadowy, willowy,
wondering
if my reflection
will be mirrored back,
knowing I exist,
unable to believe it.
Often at
the monastery,
I greet guests
as monk,
not as me,
hiding behind
the habit,
fearing visibility,
scared to be,
knowing full well
guests
must be treated
as Christ,
fearful
that this visitor
just might be.
My pretensions
skirt who I am,
two separate circles
trying to be placed
on top of each other,
they overlap
but never are one,
each circle separate,

each roundness
failing to mesh,
unable to loose
its identity
in humble transparency.

QUESTIONS

1. How fragile are you as a person? Are you afraid to share that with people? Why?

2. Write a poem that attempts to touch upon the paradoxical nature of you as a person, your strengths and weaknesses. Try to find a metaphor or simile that describes you in this state.

3. When are you most vulnerable? When least?

4. What do you see in the mirror? Is it you or is it someone else? Is the you who the world sees the you that is real?

Chapter 7

Never Too Late

[Addressing our ghosts]

I tend to be someone that can't get on with life. I often go back to the past. So therefore I am a ghosted person, someone who is surrounded by past people and events. Ghosted people are numerous. We tend to rehash the past, over and over again, ad infinitum. For example, I know a woman who lost a lot of money during the Great Depression (1929). Actually she did not loose it, but others did for her, it was her inheritance. She has lived all these years since, dragging up the past, what could have been versus what is. She lives on regrets. She harps constantly, you cannot sit with her for five minutes, without her bringing up exactly the issue of how her family lost all their money with bad investments. She has since made more money than anyone else in her family, yet she constantly goes back over the past. She has never gotten on with her life. Until she heals the past, she lives there, and can never be free to move on. Luckily I was never that bad. But certain issues have haunted me.

My mother once said to me, in her wonderful wisdom, "Can't you just go on, and not go over your real father's death?" She had. I hadn't. I was eight years old when it happened. I had taken a three week mini-sabbatical on family of origin, and addressed the issue. I was pretty sure I had addressed it. I am not someone who was mistreated or abandoned. My mother remarried three or so years after my father's death, and I could not want a better parent than my dad. He saw I was educated in good schools, was always there for me, and never beat or mistreated me. So my mother was right – "get on with your life". I had addressed the issue over and over again, but I really had never mourned my real father's death.

What I discovered is that I had some unresolved issues, and they were possibly not even real, but I had them all the same. To me these issues were real so I had to address them. I was being ghosted by the presence of my long dead father. I had this real issue of abandonment. I felt I had been deserted by him. So I had to address the issue. I realised that he did not abandon me. He died. He did not choose to die. His death was tragic at thirty-two from pneumonia, but my issues were much deeper. I had been a sleepless child, as well as a sleepless adult. I remember laying in bed the night he was taken to hospital, it is a vivid memory, a nightmare. I remember even the words being spoken. The gurney carrying him out of the apartment. Then I remember the night he died – everything – laying in bed, hearing the door open, the cry of my grandmother, my wishing it wasn't true, and so forth. Somehow I felt l was at fault for what happened. I was angry and thought I might be angry with him. I wasn't. It was God, but that will be addressed in Chapter 11. But I found that poetry released some of these resentments.

We are all ghosted by the past. We have nightmares. We have daymares. We have resentments. We have anger. Poetry affords us the opportunity to address these issues. In black and white, we realise that possibly they were not as they seemed in memory. Or maybe they weren't the way we thought but in writing we make sense of them. Ted Hughes came to grips with his wife's suicide just before his death with the statement: "Poetry is a way of talking to one's loved ones when it's too late." The point is that it is never too late. I addressed some issues in my poem on his death. It closed a door on a past event, and helped me realise my abandonment issues. But more importantly it pointed out how blessed I was with a new "dad" later and a mother who remained, during a very difficult time, always constant. My problem was I had never mourned my real father or let go of him. I did now. The poems I wrote helped me. I realise now, at this mature age, that I should have done this years ago. But I did not have the process. My mother's usual wisdom was correct, but I did not know how. This process helped me rid myself of a ghost. Unghosted I feel much more appreciative of my life, how blessed it was, and how lucky I have been. One quote that is often given is: "We become our parents." I believe that is so. When I was younger, I might not have thought that a blessing but now I do. I may have gotten some of my real father's characteristics (at least physical), some of my mother's wisdom and caring, but certainly a lot of my dad's intellectual inquisitiveness and his analytical powers. Now I can say that that is not bad. I have become my parents – all three.

Never Too Late

"Poetry is a way of talking to loved ones when it's too late."
Ted Hughes

Never saying
goodbye
has haunted
my life
since I was eight,
ghosting my adulthood
with phantoms
of a father
I never really knew.
Now at fifty-nine,
I have to talk
with someone
who died younger
than the years since,
he was only thirty-two.
What do you say
to someone who fathered you,
yet is a total stranger?
How do you approach

someone who is now mute?
How do you explain
to someone
your feeling of abandonment
when he did not opt to go?
How do you explain
your academic drive,
your doctorate,
to a man who graduated
only from elementary school?
Maybe you can't except
in fiction, in poetry,
and finally in prayer.

Hauling in the Net

"The snow was laughing: it spoke from all sides at once..."
Conrad Aiken, *Silent Snow, Secret Snow*

My sleepless mind
tugs at moonlight
as I smell apricot blossoms
on a snowy night.
Unduplicated flakes
splatter the wall
with suicidal leaps,
yet slowly accumulate
into whirling dunes.
Faces flash
across waking dreams,
I count acquaintances
jumping over barriers
to enter my life,
my mind fast-forwards,
yet I rewind myself,
floating in slow motion
to tunes played
only by a wounded heart.

I pull in my life,
counting the catch,
but notice the holes
in my net, allowing
the truth to pass through,
and I recall a Zen poet's words:
"Try catching the Tempest in a net."

God Paranoid

*"But such mistrust is
the hard lesson which a generous heart learns last.
It can be long deceived."*

Britannicus

When did I learn
to mistrust,
not just the world,
but myself,
at eight
when my father died,
at fourteen
when I failed
high school science
because I refused to cheat,
at eighteen
when I tried religious life
and failed.
Is it nature
or nurture,
I can't decide,
unimportant when,
only that I am
unable to trust,
no fact lies at the heart,
no rational reason,
only I'm never certain
that anything will last.

I always wait
for the rug to be pulled out
from under my feet,
each day I wait to be zapped,
my world to fall apart,
ultimately for God to do it again,
destroy my tightly controlled world,
God never does,
but the problem is that God could,
that is enough for a person
as paranoid as me.

QUESTIONS

1. Who ghosts your past? What ghosts walk through your life?

2. After identifying these ghosts, choose one. Now ask these questions of it: What do I need to address to this ghost? What are the real issues? Can I talk to this ghost and get answers?

3. Now take that ghost and write a poem about the person or incident that might help you get in touch with this ghost. It may take several or a multitude of poems as it did for me.

4. Ghosts rise from the subconscious periodically. If one arises in thinking about the past, address it. Don't allow it to ghost your life. Have any such ghosts wandered in and out of your life? Are you afraid of them? Why?

Chapter 8

Taking Charge
[Responsibility for one's life]

It is easy to be a victim, things happen to me and are not under my control. Many of us like the victim role because it removes from us responsibility for our lives. Vowed religious in the Catholic Church find the vow of obedience to be convenient. It exonerates the individual from responsibility for what happens in their lives. At least it did before Vatican II, but now that has changed in many communities. As human beings we are all responsible for our lives. In recent years, I have started to realise that I am in charge of what happens to me or at least how I react to a situation.

A victim tends to blame others for his/her life. A victim has more to do than others because he/she works harder and others do not. The victim becomes a martyr that way, and the reader knows a martyr is hard to live with. The martyr or victim does not get an interview and it is everyone's fault except the victim or martyr. Why? Because it is easier to blame others than take responsibility for one's life. Excuses are easy, but accepting the facts and moving on is hard.

Sometimes we can be too much in charge as well. I had a trauma when I was younger where I understood my uncle to mean I was in charge of my family after my father's death, and I applied his statement to the entire world. When I finally stopped my life in mid-course, I found that I felt responsible for the university I teach at, the monastery I reside in, the people I live with, and on and on. This type of responsibility is dangerous. It says to the believer that he or she is responsible for other people's action and lives. We cannot change anyone but ourselves. I cannot control other people's actions. Yet as a saviour of the world I thought I could. I often tell my classes to be careful of the Messiah complex – you feel you can save the world. I tell them "You are not the Messiah, he came and you are not him. Anyway look what they did to him." I tell my classes that, but I do not listen to my own sound advice.

I thought I was responsible for the world. My uncle put into my brain a seed that grew. I never forgot that message – "You are in charge of your family now". It was etched in my "child brain". My child's mind still acted as if I was in charge. I had to always be on my best behaviour. I had never to make a mistake, and when I did guilt was painted on my face. I had to combat this attitude. I had to take responsibility for myself, and no one else. I no longer will allow others to run my life. I allow no one to put guilt on me. I am an intelligent and wise person who alone knows what is good for me. I listen to others and consult others, but ultimately I have to make the decisions. Will I say yes or will I say no is up to me. If I am overworked it is because I elect to do too much. I have control of my situation, of my life. The sabbatical year helped me to realise when I am gone my classes will be taught, my duties fulfilled, and life will go on. It may not be done as I would do them, but they will all get done. Sometimes even better! I am not indispensable. It actually is good not to be indispensable, my responsibility for everything and anything is in perspective. I am responsible for my duties, and no one else's. This is what I mean when I say we are responsible for our own lives – it is also taking charge of our lives. It is also part of becoming a real adult, not chronologically, but mentally and psychologically. A psychologically sound adult is in charge of his or her life. And that is what we should each aim for, maybe not accomplish in one or two years, but aim for. I know I am in this stage in my life. Slowly asserting my control of my life. Saying "No" when asked to do too much. In some ways, trying to balance a life that often becomes imbalanced. My inner child's voice wants to be accepted, so tries to tell me to say "Yes" to almost everything because people will like me. But now I listen with my adult ears, and realise I am an adult and people will accept me as I am. My poetry helps to address some of these issues.

Taking Charge

"Mankind is frail by nature. Submit to be being mortal.
You are mortal."

Jean Racine, *Phedre*

Death
forced mother
to take on the world,
anxious by nature,
loosing a husband
at thirty-two,
with two children,
and no means
of support,
her world
was turned upside down
overnight.
As the oldest child,
I was forced also
into a role,
very similar,
that made me anxious too,
as my uncle told me
"You are the man
in the family now."
I was eight.
And from that moment,
as my uncle held me
over my father's casket,
I took on responsibility
not only
for my mother, brother,

grandmother, and aunt,
but the entire world.
After fifty years,
I still feel
that responsibility.

No Longer a Victim

"All losses must be grieved."

Fr S.M. Selvaratnam, OMI

I will no longer
allow myself to be the victim,
giving others control
of my life,
permitting myself to fall
into helplessness,
walls slowly moving
inward, trapping me,
squeezing my lifeblood,
extracting joy,
creating a vacuum
in which my destructive critic
echoes off the sides
of my soul.
I have taken charge
of whatever is left
of my life,
ten or twenty years,
knocking off
my shoulders
destructive critics,
small voices
that negate everything
I do or say,
throwing them
to the ground,
stamping on their messages,

silencing even
faint whispers,
replacing destruction
with construction,
new voices
that speak wisdom,
sapiential statements
that state truths,
finally listening
not to satanic messages
but a whisper from the Deity.

Looking with the Third Person

*"God give me death before thirty,
before my clean heart has grown dirty."*
Tennessee Williams,
Something Cloudy, Something Clear

Death didn't come at thirty,
or forty, or even fifty,
instead life trudged on,
a forced march,
sometimes directionless,
a death march,
but without an end in sight.
Today I went out of myself,
an Alice in Wonderland activity,
where I could see myself
in the distance, not close-up,
more with a telephoto lens,
I had to get far enough
to see, and not be part
of the picture itself.
Much to my amazement,
the person I wanted to be
is pretty damn close
to the person I am,

putting that into black and white
affirms what I haven't been able
to say, but I can write.
He looking at me,
my third person viewing
the me who lives within,
was not unpleased,
warts and all,
I saw a me that I can
and will live with,
not perfect, but human,
not what I set out to be,
but what I have become,
and that is maybe even better,
not planned,
but spontaneously
generated.

Becoming an Adult

"The meaning is in the waiting."

R.S. Thomas

At fifty-nine,
I may be reaching for adulthood,
finally leaving adolescence,
accepting responsibility for my life,
no excuses, no lies,
giving myself permission
for successes
and even errors.
The other day
an instructor asked
"What age are you when you hear
your destructive critic's voice?"
I thought first eight years old
the year my father died,
but then I rethought

that possibly I was
fourteen years of age
struggling with who I was
and where I was going,
afraid and too sensitive,
hearing everywhere
negative voices,
real and unreal.
These voices
are still sounding,
keeping me from enjoying
what accomplishments
come my way.
Now I may have the courage
to resist the voices,
an elusive courage,
some days I even believe
adulthood
may not be too far off.

QUESTIONS

1. Are you in charge of your life? If you are why, and if you are not, why aren't you?

2. What would it take to put you in charge of your life? Really in charge?

3. Do other people "ring your bell"? In other words, do other people get to you and try to control your actions? How can you change that?

4. Now sit down and write a poem or develop a metaphor for what you would like to see your life to be. Try to capture a life in which you are responsible for your own actions and reactions.

Chapter 9

Psychosynthesis and Masks
[Multiple personalities in one]

Each of us has multiple people living within us. Each sub-personality is developed to cope with the world around us, the positions we need to fulfil, and the responsibilities we have taken on. The key here is "I am I; I am complex." Psychosynthesis attempts to discover the whole person, or the whole person's many parts. It actually helps us to be ourselves. If one is interested one can do readings on the subject. I find the exercise to discover the various people within me the most helpful.

I had multiple aspects of my person within me. I wore various face masks for the various jobs and personalities that were required. The word *persona*, face mask, is from Greek tragedy. The actors wore those huge face masks held on a pole to portray the gods in their plays. When the Fathers of the Church tried to define God, they said, using Augustine's thoughts, that God was three personas in one. It was not three persons, such as in personalities, that they tried to define, but rather three personas or faces of God. It is our post-Freudian Church that has made God into a person with a multiple personality disorder. But each of us has different *personas* or face masks. Each face mask or sub-personality gives me insights into who I am, but also helps me be aware that all these masks have to be brought together to make a whole me. When I act as professor I act different than when I am a monk or expert in a given subject like spirituality or classroom management. Sometimes I get them mixed up. Sometimes I respond as priest when I should be professor or expert. Each of us is very complex.

Poetry helps me get in touch with some of those sub-personalities. I struggle to keep them balanced, and understand that if I take charge of my life I also need to be in charge of my sub-personalities. It is not easy.

I think the poetry will be self-explanatory. We all know some of our own sub-personalities. This is an exercise in acknowledging who we are and what makes us that unique person.

Different gods:
4 poems gathered from my sub-personalities in psychosynthesis

*"In every corner of my soul
there is an altar to a different god."*

Fernando Pessoa, Portuguese Poet

*"Sub-personalities are psychological satellites,
coexisting as a multitude of lives within the overall medium
of our personality.
Each personality has a style and a motivation of its own,
often strikingly dissimilar from those of the others."*

Piero Ferrucci, *What We May Be*

The Monk
"Only fools seek sainthood for reward."

Nensho (1409-1482), Zen Poet

I yearn
for Oneness,
yet find aloneness
frighteningly
unbearable,
silence
speaks within,

yet noise
completes
my outwardness.
Paradox
graces my inward
quest for unity,
needing
stillness,
but motionless
I sit distracted
by nothing
but myself.
My vocation
is worn
too loosely,
often able to fall
from my shoulders,
attention turned
to something
beyond,
yet what I desire
is found not afar,
but where I am,
not distanced,
but within.
The inner eye
is blinded,
not by the light,
but in the dark.

The Professor

"Nothing stays put. The world is a wheel.
All that we know, that we're made of, is motion."

Amy Clampitt, *Westward*

Teaching
has been my love,
since twenty-one
when I entered
a classroom
and all eyes
turned to me,
although
the stage
eluded me,
the podium
did not.
In recent years,
I have been
ingested
by academia,
it ate my heart,
spitting me out
only after
having nibbled
away my freedom,
assistant
to associate,
up the ladder
I have climbed,
tenured,
honoured,
acclaimed,
but only making
me hungry
for more,
I never stopped

to see
I had lost
my soul,
I wasn't,
but my career was,
I went from
Father
to Doctor.

The Poet

"Come, see real flowers of this painful world."
Basho (1644-94), Zen Haiku poet

I speak
in metaphor:
stones
weep,
seashells
birth Venus,
trees
armed human.
Poems
consume me,
eating into
my mind
so that
I produce
sentences
that beg
ownership,
breathed
into existence
from beyond,
god messages,
meaning
beyond my grasp.

I live in fear
I may expose
too much,
or reveal
too little
or maybe
something I cannot
retrieve,
namely, myself.

The Expert

"The strange and wonderful are too much with us."
Amy Clampitt, *Westward*

Years ago
I coined
the words
Video Divina,
instantly I became
an expert
on using
videos
for spiritual viewing,
I have knack
for that,
coining a word
or starting a trend,
I've done that
too many times
to be counted.
I made spirituality
relevant
even
at a national convention,
later I applied
special education techniques

to religious formation,
as did Catholic bashing,
Catechetics and responsibility,
and even homiletics
as a topic
for national magazines.
But each creation
seems to take
on a personality
of its own,
my ideas
take forms
not only outside of me,
but that are often
beyond who I am,
I become an authority
even when I don't
feel like one.

Sharps and Flats

"...if a writer still has a personality,
it is full of sharps and flats at odds with the
tuned melody emitted by his writing."
Edmund White, *The Farewell Symphony*

The persona
I project on paper
conjures up magically
someone closer
to who I am, yet
never unmasks
the hidden stranger,
a lone ranger minus the hero,
more the anti-hero,
struggling against odds,
winning only to loose ultimately.

How I create
my world differs completely
from fellow onlookers,
the picture seems
somehow all wrong,
the colours off,
the paint chipped and cracked,
unclear, maybe fogged,
an unintentional impressionist
attempt, but more surrealistic.
I compose dirges,
requiems not for me,
but for the past,
or psalms for the future,
nothing for the present,
now holds no images,
it is a vacuum, empty,
only a net for catching *déja vu*,
experiences never good enough,
shadowy songs,
dreamscapes of fantasies
that never match
the experience,
extraordinary dreams
that become daymares
once reached.

My Life on the Stage

"A performer at the circus has no theatre-curtain
to come down and hide him and thus preserve the magic
of his act unbroken."

Christopher Isherwood, *A Single Man*

Fantasy
sometimes
is more real
than reality,

I often wonder
what is real,
and what is act,
not just in myself
but in others as well,
lacking trust
in what is seen,
giving less
credence to the unseen.
My makeup
is cracking,
caked on too thick,
a mad attempt
to disguise my "I"
with a persona
totally out of character,
yet one which
seldom is detected.
I have become
astute at impersonation,
taking on characters
never in a play,
at least not one
by Williams or Shakespeare,
the problem
is the play never ends,
the curtain not drawn,
instead the drama
becomes muddled,
the protagonist
never sure when
acting is required,
and when it is not.

QUESTIONS

1. What are some of my sub-personalities? Are they based in doing or in feelings? How do I define myself and the complexity of my being?

2. Take a sub-personality and try to create a poem that captures that identity. Write from the feeling. Who is this particular person?

3. Make a list of as many of your sub-personalities as you can. Then assess if any overlap. When? How? Take five and start to assess them. Maybe give each one a metaphor.

4. Finally try to write a poem that expresses your own personal complexity.

Chapter 10
Myers-Briggs and the Enneagram
[Inventory insights]

Inventories can give us insights into who we are. Carefully used they help us focus on our who we are. These tests are now offered on the Internet, and with a little patience can be found under their own names or the same test with a different name. They have helped me understand myself over the years.

Myers-Briggs is steeped in Carl Jung, the Swiss psychiatrist, who gave us insights into our personalities. I have taken the test multiple times and always come out an INFJ. Each of us would be different. But for me a number of insights come to light which I often discount when I should take them into account. I am an "I" that is introverted, but I live the majority of my life as an "E" or extrovert. I didn't think much about that fact. As I slowly became more and more exhausted, burning out, and then struggling with what was wrong, I never went back to my Myers-Briggs inventory. If I had I would have seen that it was right in front of me. Then one day, a lecturer said, "He was an "I" who constantly worked as an "E" and was therefore exhausted." It dawned on me, or rather that that was me also. I taught, gave lectures at National Conventions, archdiocesan institutes, and so forth – all extrovert activities. But I was an introvert, I needed my private time and solitude, but I kept doing "E" things. So right here was a pattern of change needed to stop burning out. Also I am a strong "J" or judgmental. I tend to be critical, and must really work on that as well. Now I realise that this inventory gives me much insight into how and why I act as do.

The Enneagram is supposedly a Sufi development. There are nine basic types of personalities. As Sr Elizabeth

McNulty writes in her book, *Planted in Love*, "Simple and direct in its presentation the Enneagram provides the individual with a profound depth of insight into the mysteries of their own manner of being." One can find out fairly quickly what one is on reading a book on the topic. I am a "four" or a great Romantic. I am, if you haven't guessed, the poet type. The creative person who is unique. I tend to over-dramatise my life. It becomes a stage and my life is the number one act. I have to learn, notice in the future, how to not over-dramatise each event or crisis that confronts. I do that, and still do. I have a great feeling of abandonment as well, usually caused as in my case by the death of a parent early on. I cannot stand the ordinary – a trip to the zoo is ordinary, but to the zoo with an orchestra playing and champagne brunch that is special. I get bored easily, and need constant stimulation. All this helps me catch myself when I start to over-dramatise or find myself getting bored when I find my routine getting "rutted."

These two inventories have helped me immensely to cope with my life and understanding my "unique" attitude and my "Introverted" nature. They do not solve problems, but make me aware and thus the awareness helps me stop in mid-course exaggerations in my life. My poetry has tried to couple some of these attitudes as an INFJ and a four, but each of us has to be aware of ourselves. I can only see myself and my particular and "unique" personality.

Cryogenics of the Unconscious

"my memories... for the moment... were held on ice."
Edmund White, *The Farewell Symphony*

Understanding comes slowly,
experience often defies meaning,
without interpretation
knowledge is valueless,
memories fall into disuse,

frosted over,
life becomes glacier,
growing with our wintering,
inching over our terrain,
eventually growing gigantic,
burying us with soft flakes
amassed into murderous bulk.
I could say my emotions were iced,
chilled cubes
only thawed when convenient,
but that would be a lie,
something I no longer do,
at least to myself,
but I had learned
to refrigerate them,
cooling them
to a controllable degree,
hot became lukewarm,
and often cooled down,
some even gained
freezer temperature,
but not all.
Iced memories serve up
better when frozen,
melted down they go limp,
lose life, even meaning.
Sometimes numbing is necessary,
anaesthetically treating the hurt,
until healing starts, then the wound
can be reopened, but cautiously,
unfrozen, thawed, revisited,
now adding meaning to the experience.

Imploding One's Depths

"Then I imploded."

Robert Dessaix, *Night Letters*

Implosion
is a dangerous thing,
many of us
explode,
but there are a few,
like myself,
who implode,
blowing myself
inside out,
the technique may be fine
for knocking down buildings,
blowing deep mines,
but hard on human interiors.
The problem
is depth charges
are hard to control,
they have to be set
just right,
or else the implosion
destroys not just what one wanted,
but everything in the general vicinity,
on the other hand, if done probably,
the explosion destroys exactly
what one wants,
it's a risk, a gamble,
but it can do the job.
Implosion is a way to go
into the unconscious,
but you better know what
you are doing, or else
the charge may be your last.

God Revealing Commonality

"Death is the mother of beauty."

Wallace Stevens

There were
six of us,
Enneagram fours,
Romantics,
"authors", "poets",
creative persons,
three from India,
one from Indonesia,
one from Africa,
and myself
from America.
We were special,
from birth different
from our classmates,
not fitting anyone's mould,
but in meeting
we discovered how
similar our experiences
had been:
lonely, misunderstood,
at odds with our superiors,
asked to do creative things,
but often not respected
for doing what we were asked,
even feared for uniqueness,
and finally abandoned,
both then and now.
Each had suffered
from this feeling of abandonment,
death robbed two of us
of our fathers while young,
another lost her parents,
while another was left alone

for long periods of time,
each finding not powerlessness,
but strength in these occasions,
pain yes, but an inner core
that grew stronger,
like Tchaikovsky who
wrote symphonies etched
in pathos, or Merton
who found God amid
his parentless youth,
so we too had
suffered in order
to bring about
a lonely creativity
that expressed
in blood
what we experienced
in childhood,
life was lonely,
but we could create
something beautiful
out of our woundedness,
something beyond
self, namely
"art" etched
in our hurt,
coloured in torment,
twinged words
smarting agony,
finally articulating
what others cannot say,
namely,
the Deus Absconditus,
God invisible in our midst,
we could pierce
the Cloud of Unknowing,
parting fog,

and just for an instant,
reveal the face of God
and not die.

The Great Romantic

"The great romantics always live alone since a long run
can only dull the perfection of the opening night."
Edmund White, *The Farewell Symphony*

I always expect
an event
to be better
than it ever is,
I plan it in my mind,
rehearsing
what I will say
and even how
the evening
will unfold,
practising lines
that will never be said,
until the experience
that occurs
is only *déja vu*,
never good enough,
lacking in spontaneity
from mental repetition.
I always wanted
a princess
to capture my heart,
carry me off
like a fairy tale,
my girlfriends were
never good enough,
lacked something,
not measuring up
to my rigid standards.

This attitude did not go
away with adulthood,
friends, confreres, even family
do not fulfil my dreams
of what my world should be,
everyone falls short
of my romantic tale
told by a fool,
set in the mythical kingdom
of my mind.

Ordinary Existence

"Everyday... was like a day in a novel
– animated by observations, economical, eventful, intended –
and not like the slow ether drip of ordinary existence."
Edmund White, *The Farewell Symphony*

I shadowbox
boredom,
punching the air,
filling the vacuum
created by my need
to be special,
looking for emotional highs,
the latest play,
an award winning movie,
the ultimate piece of fiction,
anything to ward off
the terminal ennui
I see holding captive
the people that often
surround me.
Each weekend,
I find something
that is extraordinary to do,
I run not from myself,
but to something –

a film that may touch my soul,
a bookstore that stocks
Japanese novels in translation,
or French poetry in the original,
an art exhibit that no one else
has seen or cares to,
some insight may be gained,
a heavenly voice break through
to touch or enliven my soul,
mostly it is emptiness,
but sometimes it is a painting
that speaks beyond its colours,
a film that makes me cry
for I see my own struggle,
or a seascape that goes
from my head into my heart,
and then enraptures my soul.

QUESTIONS

1. Find the tests on Internet or in a book, and find out who you are on the inventories. Then see if it fits. Do they? Why?

2. Now try to write a poem that captures your feelings as your Myers-Briggs or Enneagram number tells you. See if the experience gives you any insights into who you are.

3. Work on your mindsets according to your inventories. Do you have a strong mindset, in other words do you act predictably. Why? What could you do about it?

4. Are you an introvert or an extrovert? How do you work with that? Do you do more out of your opposite? What do you need?

Chapter 11

Traumas and a Dialogue
[Death, abuse, and other issues]

This is the most difficult chapter to write. It is the chapter where you have to confront the traumas that often destroyed a part of your life, but it is also the most healing chapter in the book. Until we confront those traumas that have derailed our lives or created critical voices that have haunted our existence for years, we cannot go on with our life and continue the healing necessary for a healthy life.

Like every person who picks up this book and reads it, I too have had traumas, some real and some over-dramatised. I too have to fight off critical voices or destructive critics who undermine all I do with their insidious voices that tend to destroy our lives. I have voices that say "You are no good", "you can't..." or "you will fail at..." When asked whose voices they are I was often afraid to say, and so I had to force myself to address this issue of destructive critics. It was not my mother's. She has always been supportive. It was not my dad's for since he married my mother he has been a wonderful father. And my real father's I could not remember well. So who was it? One was my first Abbot who had been extremely critical of me. I had to address this man for all he had said to me. He criticised me constantly. So my destructive critic was certainly his voice, and had to be silenced. I have included a very personal poem that I wrote to address this issue – I find that it was necessary for my own health as well it might be for most of my readers.

I also needed to do the chair exercise where you put a person who hurt you into a chair (imaginary) and talk to that person and tell him what you feel and why. My life has in reality been very good, but I thought I might be angry with God. St Teresa of Avila had been angry with God and told him often about her anger, so why couldn't I? So I put God into the hot-seat. I talked with God and I asked him to explain to me what he had done in my life that I might not have agreed with. The explanation was wonderful and the first time I felt a great relief. A great stone was removed from my heart. I have included these painful poems because even if you can't write them, you can read mine, and possibly that might help. This is the most painful chapter, but also the most healing.

Facing Crisis

"Every time you face a crisis in life, there is something to be learned from it."

Julian Sleigh, *Crisis Points*

As snow devils
pirouette around me,
my snow chained
1967 mustang
is embedded in the snow,
while a stuck traffic light
burns a demented red
across my face,
I make a vow
to myself not to live
the rest of my life
in a wintry Chicago.
The crisis passed,
but the determination remained,
and eventually I transplant myself
into a world
where roses sometime
bloom in December,
and Spring comes in February,
not May.

But like all promises
it took time,
many another crisis,
multiple events transpiring,
linked together until
forcing me to take responsibility
not as God, but myself,
transplanting, uprooting,
eventually controlling
this small life of mine.
I stand once again
at a crossroads,
multiple paths in front of me,
even more behind,
I face my future
wondering what
to do
with the remaining years.

Long Silences

"My life was marked by long silences."
A.E. Housman in *The Invention of Love* by Tom Stoppard

My life
could be said
to be a series of traumas –
a father's death,
the death of a cousin from leukaemia,
a critical Abbot,
and on and on.
Yet each episode
has been marked
by triumph not defeat,
each event allowed me
the opportunity to grow,
slowly, but with strength,
something broke, but like a bone,

it came back stronger,
I am more durable,
less prone to break a second time.
Throughout my life
I have accepted these traumas
as challenges,
but now I realise that
scar tissue has built up,
I need to revisit some traumas,
maybe rebreak the event,
open up the wound,
and this time cauterise
the episode so I can go on with life.
The long silences
must be broken,
a clarity of vision established,
so that harmony
can once again reign.

Chronicling a Monastic Trauma

"... and went with half my life about my ways."
A.E. Housman in *The Invention of Love* by Tom Stoppard

When something happens
in my life, I often go on,
do not turn back,
but forge ahead,
a trauma is not addressed,
rather I ignore it
and certainly its impact,
I learned this early in life,
and sadly have not put aside
the things of childhood.
I have been a monk
for twenty-two years,
having entered in 1976,
I was twelve years

under one Abbot
before I fled to sanity,
leaving behind
family, friends, and students
in the mid-West
in order to start a new life
in Washington State.
This man
criticised all I did,
and that destroyed my self-confidence.
I entered the monastery
at 36 years of age,
a successful teacher,
awarded and rewarded
for my work with students,
a person with bachelor
and master degrees,
taking a step into
what I felt was to be
a vocation enrichment,
a monk-teacher
and possibly a priest,
but I never envisioned,
luckily, what this step
would actually mean.
From the moment,
I entered the monastery,
the Abbot decided
that I was too proud,
and life became a series
of humiliations,
an attempt to destroy
my personality,
actually me.
First my language
was imperfect
in his estimation,

I had a Chicago accent,
I said "melk" for "milk",
he would spend hours
undermining my confidence,
telling me I did not have any intelligence,
if not in words in actions,
had I not studied French,
I had, but he had taught it,
one day, he corrected seventy words
he said I had mispronounced
while table reading,
endlessly correcting and putting down
anything I said or did.
One day, I was thurifer,
I didn't hold the thurible correctly,
I did not stand right,
I walked wrong, nothing was right
about me, everything I did
was wrong or worse impossible.
Publicly he would humiliate me
so that eventually I dreaded
any community event,
my shoes were wrong,
I wore my habit incorrectly,
I rolled up my sleeves
which he publicly pulled down
two or three times,
informing those around me
that I was a disobedient monk,
he would tell me a week before
that he had something he wanted
to say to me, and then tell
me he was too busy to see me,
and hold me in suspense
for that week.
I started to write poetry out of the pain,
one of my instructors said

"Send it out to publishers",
I did, and it was published,
the following year a book
was published, and
a new source of tension grew,
my poetry and short stories,
and even articles started
to draw attention to me
and eventually I was told
"You may not write poetry",
but later after the Council
told him he couldn't do that,
he said to me
"I said I preferred
if you didn't write poetry."
My health deteriorated –
I had an ulcer
which he informed me
he was absolutely not
responsible for,
my nerves were a shambles,
eventually I dreaded
the morning,
only my teaching allowed
me to continue,
finally a doctor told me
that if I hoped to live
beyond the next few years
I probably should consider
going somewhere else.
I asked the Abbot
if I could apply for a Campus Ministry
position,
he said "Yes",
and he added,
"You can but you won't get anything",
I did and had three offers of interviews

in one week and two more the next.
I went to the interviews –
Washington, Iowa, and Pennsylvania,
and was offered two positions at the
    interviews,
something that helped me realise
that this was the route to go,
when I returned and told him,
he said I could not take the positions
because he would have to hire
three and a half people to replace me,
I was broken, I had to get out,
eventually the Council said
I could because he had given me
permission when I went on the interviews.
I choose a Benedictine monastery
to go to and live within,
but previous years have haunted
my very existence even there,
now I must face this man
because I suffer still
from the voices
which he implanted
into my psyche,
telling me I am not
good enough,
nothing I do is sufficient,
now I realise that
until I address
this issue
I cannot go on,
my monastic journey,
my life is on hold,
it is a trauma
I cannot ignore.

A Dialogued Inquisition:
Putting God on Trial

"Your hands are touching the answer."

Richard Zimler, *The Last Kabbalist of Lisbon*

ME: Could I ask you, God, to take the hot seat? I'd like to ask you some questions dealing with how you treated me as a child. I realise that your memory may not allow you to remember individual incidents since you have so many lives you are responsible for. Thank you.

GOD: Quite alright. I'll try to remember what I can.

ME: Why did you traumatise me so much when I was young? My father's death, my mother's illness, my difficult puberty, my health problems, and so forth. I felt overwhelmed, abandoned, persecuted.

GOD: How do you want me to handle this, as one issue, or each one separately?

ME: As you wish, you're God.

GOD: Your father had had tuberculosis earlier so his lungs were weak, and he caught pneumonia from over-work and not taking care of himself. I had given him as each of you free will, and he chose to abuse himself. His health was poor the final illness was too much for him.

ME: But I needed him. You left me without a father and with a mother who found it hard to cope.

GOD: Excuse me, but I provided. Your mother grew in strength, eventually growing stronger, and taking charge. I gave you a new father when you were eleven who was kind and helpful, provided for your education and your many needs. Your needs were met. But more than that what if your father had lived? His drinking was getting worse, he was absent constantly from your house, and you had your mother who you were so close to. You may have romanticised how it was or could have been.

103

Maybe it would not have been as "ideal" as you thought.

ME: You may be right, but I did feel abandoned. I felt so alone as I grew up. No one understood, and I certainly didn't either.

GOD: But was that my fault. Didn't you isolate yourself. Didn't you always think yourself special. The artist. Didn't you prefer the fantasy world to reality. My interventions within your life were to bring you back to reality. Force you to prepare for the world. Pull your nose out of a book and into work. You really did not have it so bad. In fact, much of what happened only strengthened you, did not weaken you.

ME: True, but... I needed something more. I felt so alone. And sad. Sometimes I would cry myself to sleep night after night. No one seemed to understand.

GOD: But whose fault was that. You didn't reach out. People surrounded you and you were afraid to reach out. Afraid to let people know who you were. Afraid of rejection. Are you that unhappy now?

ME: No. Not really. I feel a joy in my life. Deep and abiding. A sense of accomplishment. But sometimes I wonder. I look to the past and want it different. I wish I knew then what I know now.

GOD: Don't we all. I might have skipped the creation bit. But we can't live in the past, or in the future. But the now. Even Enneagram fours can't do that. The past is over, and the future may not come, now is all there is.

ME: Did you do this to me out of love? Or was it all just an accident? Cards dealt?

GOD: It is much more complex than that. But yes, love played a major part. I am the ultimate parent. I made you a stronger person, an adult, a success. A person who can help others. Your pain has made you compassionate and caring. Your loneliness is universalised into those you help. Your poetry and articles effect hundreds, thousands of people. The pain has helped to produce this. Without it, you would not have been you, or as effective a you as you are.

ME: But sometimes I get angry. Less so each year. But I do get angry. I feel I was given the shaft, but I realise in my mind that that is not so.

GOD: But it is inside you. Why? People envy you. People would love to have half what you have. What do you want? Birth holds no promises. And life isn't fair. Look around you. You got more than your share of talent, ability, good health, and so forth. What more do you want?

ME: When you put it that way. Nothing. I have been blessed. I'm my own worse enemy.

GOD: Anymore questions? Or is the Inquisition over?

ME: Well what about the future?

GOD: Let that up to me. If you knew too much, you'd get bored and then unhappy. Let me surprise you a little.

QUESTIONS

1. What traumas have occurred in your life?

2. Can you take one and write about it, maybe not poetry, but write down what happened? Try it.

3. Now try to metaphor the experience or write it in poetic language?

4. Did that help? If it did try another... another.. another... I did, and it does help.

Conclusion

Soulpoeting and Inner Healing
[Wonder and thanksgiving]

I have entitled this work, *Soulpoeting*, because it was the only way I could articulate what this experience was for me and could be for others. It is speaking one's soul into black and white. When I started the process, I was afraid to rip open my life through introspection. The fear paralysed me. I didn't go and throw stones in the sea, and many people I know have. I didn't beat a pillow although that exercise is very good for many people. I didn't write letters to the dead, but this is pretty close. No, I wrote poems. These poems imploded within me. They loosened many ghosts who had been haunting me. I was a ghosted person, but I didn't know why or by whom. Poetry helped me explore the issues that surfaced. Am I healed? Not yet, but on the way.

Often my facilitator on this journey would say to me "What a trauma!" I would be surprised and say, "Really?" Many of the events didn't seem like traumas, rather they were the cards dealt to me, and I played them. What really happened is that I am much more aware of who I am and also aware of what I have to work on. Healing doesn't happen overnight especially after decades of hurt and pain. It happens but slowly.

Do not be discouraged when the time schedule for healing is not your own. Some issues may take years. Others may not be healed, but accepted. Awareness is not easy, nor is it an instantaneous miracle, but it is the first step toward wholeness. It all begins with a step. My journey is slow and steady, but not accomplished. I often tell people when they ask me "When will you become perfect?" "Twenty minutes after death." The answer holds for being healed. If I were perfect I would be God, and I am not God, or even a god. I am a human being who has come to accept this flawed condition with relish. I was burned-out, exhausted, and without hope or relish for my life. Now I am a human being who accepts his humanness with all its imperfections. I do not expect to be "whole" immediately, but each day I am struggling for completeness. I often tell people who want success each day and look at spirituality as a ladder to God that for each step forward we take a mini-step backward. We make progress, but God is in charge not us.

I have found the journey humbling. The poems I shared in this book were all written in England during my sabbatical year. There are at least fifty more poems which did not make the book. That is ok because these poems were not written for publication, but for my journey. But later I was asked by many of my friends and people I shared these poems with to publish them. I felt the only way they could be published is as they were written as a journey to wholeness. I soulpoeted my way back to health, healing many aspects of myself, allowing God to touch my being with healing presence.

God has truly blessed my life and continues to. Life has not been easy, but it was never impossible. Each of us can soulpoet ourselves into a more healthy situation. Not necessarily alone. We need a soulcompanion or soulfriend to help us. If we are lucky we can find a person who is both therapist and soulfriend, but most of us will have to have the two separate. Spiritual direction is a lost art. It is needed, maybe in a different form, but it is needed.

Each of our journeys is unique. These poems may help others. It did help me. Soulpoeting gave meaning back to my life. It made me focus on what was important. Finally, it put me back in touch with God. God had gone nowhere, it was I who, to paraphrase Meister Eckhart, who was out for a walk. Soulpoeting focused me back to what was important – the gift of life I was given is the gift I have given.

These poems came not from me, but from inspiration, or as the Hebrews say *"ruah"*, the breath, the breath of God. Amen.

Fogged Windows: A Rainy Meditation

"Life's bitter jest is hollow."

R.S. Thomas

Rain
staccatos the pane,
steamed by breath,
two airs, in and out,
kiss window,
touching reflections invisibly,
see-through but opaqued.
I sit trying
to control my breath,
attempting to defog
the glass
through self-control,
frustration turns into defeat,
I cannot control "ruah",
it seeps out,
living requires breath,
only death does not.
I accept humanness,
I gulp in defeat,
yet victorious,
I am.
Paradoxically,
I open the window,
both breaths evaporate,
clarity returns,
visibility shows
beyond the glass,
I am now reflected.

Reading God's Map in My Hand

For Fr Thomas Pallichankudyil

*"... I do wake up feeling desperate to be companioned,
to feel present with someone kind."*

Robert Dessaix, *Night Letters*

I asked
you to read my palm,
make sense out of the lines,
the rivulets running off
the main streams,
the wrinkles from old age,
unravelling the string
before it is cut.
Immediately,
I sense it is not
a joke for either of us,
I wonder, question,
need a direction
after sixty years,
I don't receive a map,
I wasn't expecting one,
but it is closer to an assurance
that I am on the right path,
some may doubt,
but the lines are from God,
etched into my hand
before birth,
a child's mark
bestowed before time,
it is like a small child
that has his ear
next to his baby sister's mouth
to see if she will talk about
God having just come from heaven,
my hand is stamped
with a pattern I can't read,

but maybe you can,
seeing in my palm
an invisible story written in hieroglyphs
when I touched fingers with God.

Playing My Hand: Giving My Seminar Paper

"A poet and a scholar is what I was told."
Charon to A.E. Housman in *The Invention of Love* by Tom Stoppard

I stand before 80-plus faces,
eyes riveted on me,
then something copacetic happens,
each eye seems
to penetrate my soul,
I feel as if invisible arms
are holding me up,
fear is banished,
I feel as if I have something
to share that is larger than me,
my experience is valid
not just for me, but
for every person in the room.
At birth, I was dealt a hand,
I never asked for different cards
or even new ones,
I have played the cards
I was given,
and for the first time
that is alright,
and moreover
I have played those cards,
not just "good enough"
as some psychologists say,
but pretty damn well,
in fact very well.
For the first time in my life,
I am proud of who I am

and what I have become.
I didn't give up,
but instead I have had
the courage to fight
and make a life
that on my demise
I will be able to say
to my Creator,
"I have taken these cards you dealt me,
and here is what I have produced."
Today I realised that will be "good
enough",
and I felt enveloped by peace.

Puffs of Smoke on the Seashore

"People floated by like puffs of smoke."
                    Robert Dessaix, *Night Letters*

Fog landscapes terrain,
creating ghostly images,
a fun-house mirror
that distorts, refracts,
hides the seen in mist,
yet makes the unseen
visible by shrouding
into shape puffs of smoke.
People glide through
landbound clouds,
parting God's exhaled breath,
floating through
landed cumulus, deadly images
returned to earth,
haunting spectres
ambulating without feet
into a world minus form.
Spring heralds oblivion,
enshrouding the seacoast

with nebulous air,
allowing couples walking
the coast to play
hide-and-seek
in close proximity,
stealing a kiss
hidden by clouds,
cupid shooting arrows
without a set destination,
palling a death
metaphored in abandonment,
lost in closeness,
covered in smoke.
Only on the bay
is reality dream,
and dream reality.

Renoir's Last Painting

Nenette had gathered anemones
for beside your sickbed
while the sun slit the sky,
and as you lay in bed,
too weak to leave it,
you asked for your paintbox,
and for several hours
you become the flowers –
buttercup sunlights canvas,
lemon light across your face,
pain is forgotten.
Your petrified hand
rigidly curled inward
grips the brush,
afraid to let go,
knowing when you do
it will be forever.
When you drop the brush,

your head falls to the pillow,
and filled with awe you whisper
"I think I am beginning
to understand..."

QUESTIONS

1. Has this process of soulpoeting been helpful? If so, how?

2. If you didn't write poetry but just read, are you considering writing poetry?

3. What was the best thing about this book? What was the worse?

4. Do you feel the healing process has started? If so, why? If not, why not?

APPENDIX

I have included three articles that I have written in an appendix that might be helpful. One appeared in 1985 in *Review for Religious* entitled "Contemplata Tradere: The Presence of God in the Ordinary". It includes my first poems. The reaction to this article planted the seeds over a decade ago for this book. I received more responses to this article than anything I have ever written. Mother Generals used poems from the article to open chapters, I made friendships with women who still write me from all over the world (India, Peru, Africa), and finally I believe that these poems helped people heal their lives.

The second article appeared in *Spiritual Life* in 1996 and is entitled "Soul-Speaking: Spiritual Friendship". Again the article was amazingly received. It was regularly read in a Protestant seminary in Pennsylvania. A number of authors of books on Spiritual direction wrote me, and finally it again is a practical application of what I didn't know would be this book.

The third article was never published, but was produced for a class in spiritual direction during my doctoral programme at San Francisco Theological Seminary. Sr Beth Liebert allowed me to do a fictional paper for the course, and this is the end result. I shared it with the class, and it inspired many to write poetry.

Contemplata Tradere:
The Presence of God in the
Ordinary

A Butterfly's Kiss
"... the blue dome of the mountain sky was as pure as the
Lord's pain..."

Peter Matthiessen

On television recently, there was a special on the Amazon
    and its multitudinous inhabitants both within
    and around its river banks.
The announcer was matter-of-factly showing us
    tapirs mixed with cockatoos, and even
    river creatures seen from underneath-something
    only a photographer would understand.
Yet as he droned on, and scene after scene paralleled,
    my mind wandered with him, but I never left
    the room.
And then a most amazing thing occurred: he announced,
    much like the Archangel, that we were now
    seeing a butterfly kiss away the teardrops
    of a river-swimming turtle, and although
    he mentioned
    it was for the salt, my mind just soared away.
A river where a butterfly kisses turtle tears away
    was a special place found only in the
    kingdom of God where anything was now possible.
Just imagine such a princedom – it boggles all thought
    where even prehistoric turtles would be sad for only a
    short time.
    There the hurt would all be healed
    by one soft, tender kiss – butterfly implanted

lips so soft you couldn't feel them, yet strong
    enough to suck away even your fear.
So here was a place, somewhere in Brazil, where,
    when I was really broken and feeling no hope,
    I could board a plane for Rio and have butterflies
    kiss my cheeks.
Now I know I'll never visit this jungle in Brazil,
    but at least I can hope that someday these
    creatures may migrate. And then walking down
    a street one morning, tears streaming from my eyes,
    a butterfly may swoop down and kiss my
    tear-stained face.

An Epiphany in a Thorn Tree

This dawn as I meditatively took a stroll
    I promptly was enthralled by a buzzing tree.
The sound took me totally by surprise
    and left me with a constant yet disturbing note.
As Moses was met once by his God in a burning bush
    so I was confronted by my God in a cockspur
    hawthorn tree.
The tree was full in bloom – snowflaked white
    with blossoms opened beyond their capacity,
    waiting to be brushed away by God's gentle breath
    or his soft tear-like rain.
Yet through these blossoms poked pain-filled thorns
as fearsome as those around the sacred head.
And between the placid blossom and the awesome spear-
    like thorn
    were bees, hundreds of bees, hovering over each petal.
The tree was alive with bees contentedly working out
    their existence between blossom and thorn,
    seemingly unaware of any plan except to gather
    in the sweetness of the Lord.

I could not help but pour myself into this tree,
    and see how often we gather in the honeyed
    gifts of God
    so often unaware of the danger surrounding
The cockspur hawthorn was a burning bush
    yet it had no fire,
    only sound to attract this viewer to his God.
A tree alive with buzzing bees
    brought me closer to a truth:
    Man is not in charge of God's appearances,
    God alone manifests himself where he wills.
Soft petals soon to disappear,
    sharp thorns to remain in perilous tact,
    and bees filled with nectar leaving for hives unknown.
Yet God came and showed himself in that hawthorn tree
    no burning bush was needed
    He appeared within his own nature
    freely and luckily unhampered by me.

Three Mystical Love Poems
Based on Hildegard of Bingen

First Love

"For God is love."

John 4:8

It happened in one providential moment.
  We had made love with our eyes before,
  yet we were unsure, unsafe.
  Fear. Uncertainty. Mistrust.
Our eyes drew us together,
  then lips brushed,
  then they touched,
  then we knew.
In one risk, your passion charged my being,
  and made me know God.
  Fear fled. Years vanished. Hiding ceased.
Someone knew who I was
  and still loved me.
We became lovers, yet much more.
  We became love.
  Fear and loneliness were dead,
  and now we knew God in love
  and so are we.

You Are So Beautiful

*"Let us make man in our image,
after our own likeness.."*

Genesis 1:26

Michelangelo could create from a block of stone a
  perfect man,
  a sculpted David.

The stone seemed to take on life,
  but, lacking breath, it remained stone.
For Michelangelo was a great artist, not God.
  His talents only mimicked his God.
Yet the beauty he created is awesome and lasting.
  And even today his David stands amid Florentine
  treasures.
Now God creates in human flesh and bone,
  and breathes a soul within a man.
  He moulds and shapes,
  scrapes and buffs and even hurts,
  and finally stands back and allows to grow.
God makes us the way we are,
  no regrets, no excuses, just us.
And then he whispers, through a love's voice:
  "You are so beautiful. I love you.

Sure in an Unsure World

"Jesus asked, 'Do you love me?'

John 21:17

Maybe Jesus too felt insecurity when he loved
  and even feared being unloved and rejected.
  So why shouldn't I who am so insecure
  need to know whether I am loved or not.
Fear dwells in my heart and eats at my brain
  "Why should anyone love me?"
  and no answers come to mind.
Yet someone loves me
  His body tells me so,
  His eyes yearn for me,
  His kisses eat my soul.
Maybe I'm too insecure to ever be able to fully love
  but I'm trying, trying not to possess.
So I ask the question daily, too often
  "Do you love me?"

and pray to hear "Yes, you know I do."
Fear then is banished and love fills my soul,
    and I know once again I'm loved for who I am.
Yet my heart knows I cannot hold captive
    someone as beautiful as you,
    but our love is as sure in an unsure world
    as love can be.

Our Owner's Voice

"...and they shall hear my voice..."

John 10:16

In many ancient societies, it was rumoured
        shepherds could
control their lambs with but a flick of their voice,
    and no lamb could escape the beckoning tones
        from such pastoral herdsmen.
    Jesus himself used such a pastoral image,
        and even called him Good,
sending out this man in search of one lost sheep.
    Yet sheep are really smelly creatures,
        often hard for strangers to control,
    and not at all prone to animal aristocracy.
So once again we've taken what Jesus was trying to say,
and domesticated his words by black-and-whiting them
        into yesterday's good news.
    It is so easy to miss this story's point
        and heaven help us if we do
    the Good Shepherd wasn't what he did
    but who he was in pursuing his sheep.
Most of us do not know a lot about sheepfolds:
    we tend to picture lambs as something from which
        we get wool,
and only on a country ride do we envision sheep afar off
    and hygienically sealed by squeeky-clean car windows
        framing their white contours.

121

Yet sheep for all their foulness and temperamental quirks
have one characteristic which sets them apart from us:
a lamb knows his owner's voice, and hears his call.
Now God whispers to us like little lambs every second
of the day,
and unlike the parabolic sheep our ears are waxed shut,
so now we each must try to open up
and listen to his voice,
a master calling for his sheep,
a lamb who is very lost.

Review for Religious (1985)

Soul-speaking:
Spiritual Friendship as a Possible Model for Spiritual Direction within the Parish

If my own religious experience has followed in the footsteps of many other Catholics, I have found it extremely difficult to find a spiritual director. Even in the seminary, I found good spiritual directors few and far between, and therefore went without one frequently. And since that time, I have had the ongoing struggle of finding someone to help guide me through mid-life crisis. I think part of the problem lies with what we are looking for in a spiritual director and often what we are expecting from that same person. I realise there are no "absolute" answers, yet with pastors, sisters, and parish personnel so busy, I would like to posit an alternative to spiritual direction, or maybe better a solution to this problem at least for some of us. This article is an attempt to look in a somewhat different direction for a spiritual "mother" or "father" – looking instead to "spiritual friendship "as the source of our guidance and growth in the Lord. I call this approach "soul-speaking".

"Soul-speaking" might best capture what a spiritual director and his or her directee may be doing in what is traditionally called "spiritual direction". This intimate union of two souls has been touched upon by many spiritual writers throughout the centuries, including Aelred of Rievaulx, Catherine of Sienna, and Thomas Merton in more recent years. They have all fingered the topic and left their prints, but when all is said and done I do not believe that any have touched upon the hermeneutics of spiritual direction with the exception of Aelred. And this failure by most authors has left a gap in the literature written for the direction of souls. Most writers talk about a spirituality of direction, or about psychological aspects of directing a person, or may even touch upon the role of the Holy Spirit. But few writers have dealt with spiritual direction as a relationship based on and in friendship. I would like to explore such relationships or the pursuit of God within a relationship which includes spiritual direction. I could find no word which really expressed this concept of spiritual friendship/ direction so I coined the phrase: "Soul-Speaking." I believe that only when two souls are in total and complete communion does a spiritual intercourse take place in which the two individuals openly bear their souls to each other in such a way that they are one with the One. Now this may sound very romantic but I do not believe so. Instead I will even take it a step further that only two souls in love with God and with each other, in the purest of sense, can in reality grow in the Lord, and stretch each other in true spiritual direction.

The language of spiritual direction has for years been grounded in "theological jargon", or different stages of development which aim through a series of steps toward arriving at God. From Origen through Gregory of Nyssa, and on through the medieval writers, William St Thierry and even Bernard of Clairvaux, they all had steps or ladders which have been used to symbolise the ascent to God, for the spiritual quest was usually seen as an ascent. Such a process was imposed on the directee with rigour, and the end result was a rigid structure which sometimes was thought to earn salvation. Then in the post-Vatican II renewal, psychology became the "god" for the spiritual quest. Often the spiritual director was more psychologist than spiritual adviser. And terms were bantered about as if it were a session rather than direction. Now I think that we have reached a period when we need a new approach. "Soul-speaking" moves us into the realm of friend as spiritual director or spiritual director as friend. For either one can occur first. I think this whole idea is rooted in the Scriptures, and an application was given to us by Aelred of Rievaulx in his classic work, *Spiritual Friendship*.

Aelred of Rievaulx (1110-1167) starts his work with a statement which is essential to any true spiritual direction: "Here we are, you and I, and I hope a third, Christ, is in our midst." (p. 51). All spiritual direction must take place in the presence of God, but not just in the presence but in the acknowledged presence of God. For years, authors have talked about the spiritual direction as a science, but it isn't. Spiritual direction is not a science or even an art, it is more love spilling out from one person into another. Two people sharing their stories of God. Or as Aelred puts it: "For what more sublime can be said of friendship, what more true, what more profitable, than that it ought to, and is proved to, begin in Christ, continue in Christ, and be perfected in Christ?" (p. 53). Scripture backs this up when it says in Proverbs: "He that is a friend loves at all times." (Prov 17:17). And since God is love, and love abides in God, true spiritual direction must take place within the loving presence of God. Aelred emphasises that a spiritual friendship "...is cemented by similarity of life, morals, and pursuits among the just" (p. 59). I cannot share myself with someone unless I truly trust that person, and since spiritual direction requires total risk of self that person must be a friend. Such a friendship "...is a mutual conformity in matters human and divine untied with benevolence and charity." We must love the one to whom we are committing ourselves. For only when I love can I totally commit myself to the risk involved in sharing myself. Friendship and love are mutually exchangeable according to Aelred, and I believe so when talking of real friendship. So therefore if we utilise the words of Aelred on spiritual friendship as interchangeable with spiritual director, I believe we have an important inroad into an area which I will call "Soul-speaking". This is exceptionally available in parish life because friendship can lead to deeper insights into the way God walks within our lives, yet there are some dangers inherent in this form of spiritual direction.

St Teresa of Avila warned us about choosing a spiritual director, and told us of the difficulty one will have in trying to find one. But recently during a class I taught in Christian Spirituality, a young man raised his hand, and asked "In this day and age, with so much material available in spirituality, is it necessary to have a spiritual director?" It took me back for a second. And without thinking I answered, "Yes!" And then I filled-out my answer, "Yes. We need someone to help us through the rough spots, point out our errors, and even chide us to do better." And then I blurted out, "A spiritual friend." And all of a sudden it dawned on me that what we truly need is someone to "soul-speak" with, a person to share our depth with, an individual who accepts us for who we are and then draws us to who we can become. "A spiritual friend" is just that. Now all of us trained in psychology know that true friendship is rare, maybe once or twice in a lifetime do we truly have a symbiotic relationship in which we touch souls with someone. It would be nice if it happened more often but it does not. Then what are our chances of finding a "spiritual friend" who can also act as a soul-mate or spiritual director. I think we can, but we have to look, and more importantly risk ourselves to find that special person. I wish to set down some criteria for that search, and possible a few ideas which might be helpful to a prospective directee.

In *Morning Light: The Spiritual Journal of Jean Sulivan,* the author set down one important criteria for a spiritual director, he writes that "...many are still discussing a dead man even when they think they're talking about resurrection" (p. 23). The first criteria for a spiritual director and/or spiritual friend should be that the person believe that Jesus rose from the dead. Now I know many people will laugh at this, but I mean truly believe that Jesus is alive. Not only that Jesus lives, but he walks among us. And the belief must radiate in that person's life. Not that the director must be a saint, just the opposite, she or he must be a fellow-traveller, but someone who believes that Jesus is real. Such a belief is radiated in the action, concern, and care that this person shows to those around her or him. Sulivan was right, most Christians do not believe that Jesus ever left the tomb on Easter Morn, for most he is still there.

A second criteria I would put forward is that the spiritual director be imbued with Scripture, but not exegesis or fundamentalist trivia. The two extremes are self-serving, and not self-giving. For a spiritual director, the gospels must be alive. Scripture is not something to be read with the mind, but the heart. Sulivan writes that the gospels are poems:

> ...breath, rhythm, gesture, parable, and paradox – poems – are once simple and secret, and only gradually be unveiled. A poem accomplishes what it speaks of, but through a process that is never complete. The persons who receive it must return into darkness where they will never finish exploring it (p. 22).

Now I know it seems ridiculous to maintain that a spiritual director be a poet, but it would help. Someone who speaks in metaphor. A person who is able to zap us like a parable. A storyteller who evokes from us a response on an eschatological level. Impossible? Not necessarily. Where can this sort of person be found. I believe within friendship that may possibly already exist. I know that within friendship, close personal relationships, there also exists the possibility to expand this closeness into a spiritual friendship. As I tell people if the person you are considering as your director comes in and has all the answers to all your questions, and even answers for questions you haven't asked. RUN! The spiritual quest is a mutual journey, and it is filled with doubt. And no one, even if they have walked the same road, can answer all the questions. It is a journey for those who doubt, yet remain faithful. But it is journey. And both director and directee have to be on it. It is a quest not for black and white, but rather a walk through the grey areas which most of us live our lives in.

What criteria should we use in the specific choice of a spiritual director who *is* a friend. I think the first criteria is that the person be someone who we can share exactly who we are with, and not be ashamed or fearful. Secondly, the person must be truthful with us. Able to confront us when we are wrong. Yet free enough to say whatever he or she thinks, and know we will not be offended. Thirdly, the person should love us deeply enough to remain a friend forever. As St Jerome wrote: "A friendship that can cease to exist, never was a true friendship." I agree. True friendship accepts the other without hesitation, but continues to help the other grow. Therefore real spiritual direction is mutual growth, both expanding the other.

I have found that each of us have such people in our lives. People with whom we have such an intimate relationship. For religious, it may be a fellow-member of a community, or a member of one's family. For a married person, it may be a spouse, or a life-long friend. The person we share everything with. Or it may even be with two different people. It is with this person that we share soul, become vulnerable. The day of the Jansenistic priest who tried to impose an alien spirituality on a person is hopefully gone. Today we have to explore life, and hopefully with someone who has the same goals and aims. It is not so much a necessity to be objective but rather compassionate. And age makes no difference. In this day and age, we have to see that often someone younger or much older might be the ideal person for this type of spiritual friendship.

I believe that at least one of the two people involved in this spiritual friendship should be imbued with Scripture and hopefully well read in modern spiritual writers, but not necessarily as scholar. A person who knows where to look is much more important than someone with all the answers. The key to this relationship of mutuality is to share one's self and the commonality of the human experience. Poetry works for me. I write to the one with whom I am mutually growing. The first one was written for a person with whom I had developed a friendship first, and then became a person with whom we were mutually growing in God so I wrote: "A True Sharing." It has an epigram from Galatians 6:2 – "Help one another carry these loads…"

How often in my life I've yearned to have a friend
and often planned and plotted to just such an end.
Yet such friends never really were,
    for, forced, they fled,
        and planned they rebelled
            evaporating when over possessed.
So loneliness forced me in desperation to construct
    walls and ramparts around my inner being,
    but never were these fortress barriers strong enough
        to keep out the pain of solitude.
The need to share myself and allow someone to hear
    about the me no one knew paramounted all I did.
Then one day it happened: a person entered into me
    with whom I could share myself, and never be
    ashamed.
He knew what it was to suffer, and how it was to hide.
    He never judged my statements, nor asked me why.
This friend shared himself right back, and gave me
    room to be.
    He always cared about me, and yet never tried to
    possess me.
How do you thank a person for loving without strings,
    or listening when you need someone to hear,
        or most of all freeing me to be.

For this person, this poem was a breakthrough, and for myself it was as well for I told someone how I felt which I was afraid to do orally, but could do in writing. Since that time I've learned to do it both ways. I believe poetry affords a way of speaking which often oral communication does not. I have found that my poems or even someone else's can break through barriers that allow us to talk of God or soul-speak with each other.

Another time I found a spiritual directee who needed to be reassured that he would be supported no matter what, yet was so shy of speaking openly about himself or his relationship with God. I wrote "People Shy" with an epigram from St Jerome "Friendship which can end was never true friendship".

Someday I'd like to strip away the layers of your hurt
and touch the very hidden depths walled up within
    your being.
Words will never reach within your secret cell,
    for words only echo back the hollowness within
        themselves.
If I could only open up the beauty I have glimpsed in you
    and free the gentle prisoner caught within your
        self-made walls.
Then you could freely fly wherever you would want
    but never be enclosed again by yearning for what
        is not.
My desire to touch your shyness,
    and wipe away your fears,
        is probably doomed to failure,
            because it asks too much, too soon.
Yet if I love you so completely as I do
    then this love should touch every crumbled stone
    of your now-partially broken cell,
        and may even reach your pulsating heart
            with freedom to start anew.
Maybe only two really shy people can free each other,
    for only when a person knows the loneliness within
        can he reach out and touch the other's isolation.
So we too have each other – maybe that is all we need
    at least we know someone knows and cares and loves
        and is.
Now if we share this people-shyness walking hand in hand
    then we will have a friendship that can never really end.

Such a poem or one selected from an anthology or a favourite collection, or a short story or a novel is a great breaking ground. I find that a commonality of experience is often helped by something like this. I have a number of people with whom I have a spiritual friendship and share poetry and short stories. The other night one such person stopped in the midst of a conversation and said, "Do you know we never talk of God?" And my response was "Do we have to?" He looked at me and said "No!" And then I thought of Aelred of Rievaulx's comment: "Here we are, you and I, and I hope a third, Christ, is in our midst." No need to talk of God because God is in our conversation. I guess when it is all said and done the key to any good spiritual direction is compassion. *Teleios* in Greek. "You must therefore be perfect as your heavenly Father is perfect" (Mt 5:48). That is the horrible translation of *teleios*. It is not perfect, but compassionate. A spiritual friend should be wholehearted, unreservedly committed, loving like God. J.D. Salinger in *Catcher in the Rye* captured what *teleios* meant. Holden Caulfield had been expelled from his prep school and was all mixed up. He was trying to find meaning in his life. And he recalled a line from Robert Burns, "If a body meet a body, coming through the rye," but he remembers it wrongly, "If a body catch a body," and then he mused:

> Anyway, I keep picturing all these little kids playing some game in this big field of rye and all. Thousands of little kids, and nobody's around – nobody big, I mean – except me. And I'm standing on the edge of some crazy cliff. What I have to do, I have to catch everybody if they start to go over the cliff. I know it is crazy, but that's the only thing I'd like to do. I'd just like to be the catcher in the rye.

That is what Jesus means by a love devoid of self, or compassionate. We, you and I, live in a field of rye, and our vocation as Christians is to catch people before they fall. When we soul-speak in spiritual friendship, following in the footsteps of Jesus and the spirituality of Aelred of Rievaulx, we actually spiritual direct each other in mutuality. Since spiritual directors anywhere are much less in the parish maybe this is the way to go for some of us, and if it is, then the model of Aelred might be the one to follow.

Aelred of Rievaulx, *Spiritual Friendship* translated by Mary Eugenia Laker SSND, (Washington, D.C., Cistercian Publications, 1974).

Spiritual Life (1996)

Reading Frost Ferns:
A Short Story
about Spiritual Guidance

"The important thing is not to stop questioning."
Albert Einstein

*"To die for a religion is easier than
to live it absolutely."*
Jorge Luis Borges

Sometimes nothing happens until something does. You know what I mean. A zap disrupts your life. Your cat throws up. The kid screams, "You hit me", full blast in the local supermarket as your pastor stands one aisle away. Not something catastrophic, but rather something ordinary which becomes extra ordinary. It is that soft whisper of Elijah on the mountain top. Today was such a day, but maybe I have to start at the very beginning, which as Rogers or Hammerstein, I can never keep them straight, wrote, "It is a very good place to start."

About six months ago, she walked into my office. Now that was an exaggeration for she didn't really walk in, but fell through the door, hanging on to the lintel so as not to fall. I probably should explain right now who I am, and then maybe what I am. Who always comes first. Who am I? Nothing like a little ontological thought to get the blood moving. I am not who am, but like most people I follow the reverse heliocentric theory, I usually follow as a close second to I am who am. Maybe I can best describe myself as I am who is becoming. Who am I becoming? Now that is the question. Sorry no answer. Just the one who is on a journey. To Where? Some days to nowhere, and other days to the next giant step or sometimes just a baby step. Like Bob in the Hollywood film *What about Bob?* who goes to the psychotherapist and is given a new method of therapy, baby steps, just take baby steps. Well that is me. I am the expert on baby steps. I take really tiny ones most days. So who am I? I'm a liver, not a cow's, but rather like in French, *joie d'vivre* or something like that. I live life. Each day is a new conquest. I'm the one who stands at the window in an airport and yells "Nice job, God!" when I see a sunset. Or the person sees a snowman melting and cries. Yep! That's me.

So what am I? That good old American adage, "What do you do for a living?", followed pretty quickly by "and how much do you make?" Well, when I answer no one asks the second question. Guess? I am a poet. Well, even I know no one really earns a living doing that. I can write until I am blue in the face, and when I can't pay the heating bill I am often blue or red in the face, but you and I both know of probably four poets in the whole world who earn a living as a poet, and three of those are dead. And they are earning the big bucks, while the one live poet is probably living in a garret in downtown Seattle (the in place for poet's this year). So what do I really do? I am a spiritual director. Now that is the big bucks. Stop laughing. I know you find that hard to believe, but I am a spiritual director. The people who come to me don't know it – they think I am a professional counsellor or a teacher or a person who ministers and a few may even, God forbid, think I am a poet, but probably none of the people who come to me think that I am a spiritual director. It just ain't in their vocabulary.

So who comes to the likes of me, a poet turned spiritual director? Now that is a good question, and when you've got an answer please share it with me. My only reply would be probably the people you least expect. It is sort of what Basho wrote in his haiku:

When you look carefully
I see the nazuna blooming
by the hedge.

It is the doorway through which the least probable people walk. Maybe the term which best suits this type of person who seeks me out is the psychological term "the wounded". The wounded, not necessarily the externally scared, but the interiorly wounded. The person who would be one huge scar if we had "soul" x-rays, but again it is lucky we don't because I'd have to have one, and I am the most wounded of them all.

How did I get into this position? Not by choice. I want to make that perfectly clear, and now I sound like Nixon. I never chose to be a spiritual director, it chose me, or maybe better God, she or he, grabbed me up and plunked me down in this particular area. People just started appearing at my door, and then I couldn't turn them away. What do you say, "Get the Hell out of here!" No way. So we talked, and when I didn't have answers, I frequently had to run to the local bookstore and pick up the latest books on this or that "ism". I frequently felt one step in front of the person who came to me, but that was ok since God was in charge and not me. No cop out, but the truth. I was sort of like the acoustical tile on the ceiling of my office – I absorbed a lot of the beating the person was taking, and didn't try to solve the problem, only focus it. Focus it where – on themselves, on me. No! On God. Directly do I do this. Nope. Sometimes it is a long time in coming – a couple of months, a year, and sometimes even two or three years, but eventually it turns to God. Sound a little like the twelve-step programmes from AA. It should because there is a lot of commonality, but it is more – it is a realisation that God is where we have to turn. Now you got a little background, let's go back to the beginning that very good place to start, but we can't because you really haven't met Anne yet. So let's do that first.

Anne crashed into my life about year ago. She dive-bombed into my office, exploding all over me and my desk like Hiroshima at the end of World War II. And she could remember that far back – not much further – but that far.

She was dressed in a dress that might have won the award for Pan-African design of the year – lemon yellow, plum purple peppermint green, sky blue, and a splash of acid orange. My eyes were still focusing when she spoke. Again, spoke might be a little much because it wasn't that calm, and cackle would be too chicken coopie, so I will say that she sprayed the room with her entreaty. She shocked herself. Then me. Anne isn't a big woman, but she seemed that way. She blurted out "God spoke to me last night." I sat there a second, and all sorts of things crossed my mind, "Another nut!" "Oh God, why me?" and finally, "I hope she isn't violent." She seemed to read my mind, "No, really God spoke to me last night." My only response was: "Why don't you have a seat and tell me about it?" She looked sceptical. "You don't believe me!" I feebly came forward with, "Yes, I do," but I don't believe I believed it myself, and she didn't believe me for sure. She still was standing. It was a stand-off. A minute passed. Then she sat down as if to say I got nowhere else to go so I might as well sit here.

I looked at her and for some reason I liked her. She was not physically beautiful, but there was something about her that struck me as someone who had been beaten up a lot. And I could identity with that in her. She had a hanky in her hand and she twisted it into a Chinese thumbscrew like I used to get when I was a kid at the carnival. Her hands were held captive by her hanky. I tried to catch her eye, but she was downcast to the area around her hands. Softly I said, "Do you want to tell me about it?" And then I felt the hollowness of my words, but somehow she didn't – and she started her story. Her mother had always controlled her life. She didn't remember her father, but only her mother. Now her mother was sick, and she had to take care of her, yet she felt trapped and wanted out. Yet last night something strange had happened to her. As she was changing her mother's soiled sheets, and thinking of how her life was going down the drain, her mother had looked at her and

136

said, "Anne, thank you." And for a second, a picture of Jesus flashed before her eyes, she saw the face of Jesus in her mother's face. But that couldn't be. It wasn't possible. No way! God doesn't work that way. God stays in the heavens, and Anne stays on earth. It is a fair and mutual arrangement. God may have broken the rules last night, and that wasn't kosher.

Her next question was what I would have asked, "You agree don't you that God doesn't act this way?" Now I was on the cutting block. How did I think God worked? Did he break into our lonely existences? Did God zap us when we least expected it? Did she take on the face of those around us? Is our God incarnational? Maybe I should just say, "You're right Anne. God doesn't work that way. God stays out of our lives." But I couldn't and before I knew it I said the magic words, "Why not? How does God work, Anne?" That was it. She looked as if I was the Wizard of Oz before his denouement by Dorothy. She sat there and stared at me. Finally she said, "I'm not sure." And I replied quickly, "And neither am I." And that started us on the road to exploring who we were together. It was a rough road. More bumps than smooth parts, but a road.

Like the time, she walked into my office and said, "I think I should quit my job." "Why? Because it just doesn't feel right." "Why doesn't it feel right? I should be doing more with my life than that crummy old job. I'm going nowhere." "Why?" "I want more out of life than I am getting. Look how you help people. I'd like to do that." "You could." "But I don't. What is wrong with me?" So we explored a little of what spiritual direction is about. I gave her a couple of books to read. I stressed that spiritual guidance did not require a M.A. in Spiritual Direction. Some spiritual directors like Catherine of Sienna and Catherine of Genoa were illiterate. Others were people who really loved like Aelred of Rievaulx and Francis of Assisi, and others were real pains in the posterior like Jerome. It was what God called us to and not what we did or how educated we were. She was amazed. Her thirst for God had grown over the years, and now she was realising that she was not satisfied to hold it in but wanted to share this experience with others.

Where the journey was leading Anne and me was never too clear. It was always surprising. For me, I was always learning. Often when I was through I didn't know if I was the same person as when I started the hour before. One day when Anne had had a really bad week, she recounted some of the problems with mother, her illness, and even her job. I finally said to her how do you cope, and she just looked at me, and pointed upward with tears in her eyes. She made me over and over again centre my own life on God as I tried to help her centre her life the same way.

Don't get me wrong. Anne was not pietistic, but a realist to an absolute degree. But we were on the same human journey trying to make sense of the life we had been dealt. As I always said to her, "No answers, only more questions." And she'd say, "And I got more where these came from." And yet as I introduced her to poetry she started to collect poems which meant something to me. One time in *Gypsy*, an international magazine published in West Germany, she found a poem which she said was exactly how she felt about her relationship with God. It was entitled "A Fearful Thing", and started with a quote from Hebrews 10:31: "It is a fearful thing to fall into the hands of the living God." She then read me the poem with trembling voice:

> You grab at me too tightly,
> afraid I might fall
> between your outstretched fingertips,
> a piece of lint against your palm.
> I speck your skin with self.
> You don't brush me away.
> My ego quakes with fear
> as trembling I dance across you,
> suddenly feeling the warmth of your hand.

I end up a mote
squashed by your caress,
stuck to your fist
by the sweat of passionate love.

The poem was written by some unknown author, yet the
words spoke to both of us. Our search for God was as
passionate as any love affair, and yet it was without passion.
The paradox of what we were doing in our mutual journey
became evident in one flashing moment to each of us. This
poem became our anthem.

As time went on we struggled for some symbol which
could capture what we were doing in this mutual journey
in spiritual awareness. We ran through so many symbols
and stories. All fell flat until one day, Anne again found a
poem in *RAJAH* – the *Rackham Journal of the Arts and
Humanities* of the University of Michigan. It was called
"Frost Ferns", a simple enough title, but for Anne it was
the symbol for what had happened between both of us.

Windows encrusted
with snowy fronds
made by warm breath
in an unheated room
tunnel me backward
to yesterdays, nonaged.
I sleep once more
in a dormitory
with one hundred bodies
seeking dreamed pleasure,
touching miraged desires,
yet needing much more.
Frost ferns,
born of steamy passion,
painted on windowpanes
in ice-milk patterns,
tell cobwebbed stories

predicting future nights,
revealing hidden yearnings.
Hoarfrosted glass
erased like the years
by a few degrees
of morning sunlight,
yet remaining
if cloudy and frigid
a whole day,
even a lifetime
on a latticed mind.

We sat there in silence. Then Anne turned to me and said, "We have been reading our frost ferns, our ice etchings. Our breath has created a series of delicate paintings on the windows surrounding us and we have read them. Together. And not just ours, but God's ruah or breath also. And we have had to do it quickly because the sun comes out and melts them away. That is what we have been doing – reading frost ferns."

It sort of put the whole thing into perspective. Who am I? What do I do? I read frost ferns from my very being. Not bad. There are a lot worse jobs out there. And maybe on a cold wintry day they might even remain on the windows of my life long enough to see them clearly, but then why? Why? Why? I've a lot of questions, but the answers just don't come.

Bibliography

Duncan, Bruce, *Pray Your Way: Your Personality and God*, London, Darton, Longman and Todd, 1998.

Egan, Gerard, *The Skilled Helper*, Pacific Grove, CA, Brooks/Cole, 1998.

Ferrucci, Piero, *What We May Be: The Vision and Techniques of Psychosynthesis*, London, Thorsons, 1995.

Fischer, Kathleen R. *The Inner Rainbow: The Imagination in Christian Life*, New York, Paulist Press, 1983.

Fox, John, *Poetic Medicine: The Healing Art of Poem-Making*, New York, Putnam, 1997.

L'Engle, Madeleine, *Walking on Water: Reflection on Faith and Art*, New York, Bantam, 1980.

McManus, Jim, *Healing in the Spirit: Inner Healing and Deliverance in Today's Church*, London, Darton, Longman and Todd, 1994.

McNulty, Elizabeth Welsh, *Planted in Love: The Enneagram Reasoning and Conversion*, London, St Pauls, 1995.

Myers, Isabel, *Introduction to Type*, Palo Alto, CA, Consulting Psychologists Press, 1980.

Prest, Layne A. and James F. Keller, "Spirituality and Family Therapy: Spiritual Beliefs, Myths, and Metaphors", *Journal of Marital and Family Therapy*, Vol. 19, No. 2, 137-148.

Sanford, John A. *Evil: The Shadow Side of Reality*, New York, Crossroads, 1987.

Stewart, Ian and Vann Joines, *TA Today: A New Introduction to Transactional Analysis*, Nottingham, Lifespace Publishing, 1987.

Webb, Karen, *The Enneagram*, London, Thorsons, 1996.